Citizenship Schools

A practical guide to education for citizenship and personal development

Titus Alexander

---

*Adding wings to a caterpillar
does not make a butterfly.*

Dr Stephanie Pace Marshall

---

*Education shall be directed to the full development of
the human personality and to the strengthening of
respect for human rights and fundamental freedoms.*

Article 26 (ii), Universal Declaration of Human Rights

Acknowledgements

Above all, I would like to thank the pupils, teachers, parents, schools and community groups from whom I have learnt everything described in this book. I would like to thank Simon Richey for encouraging me to write it down, and for his constructive comments on the text. My thanks also go to the Gulbenkian Foundation, without whom it would not have been written, the Campaign for Learning and UNICEF, without whom it would not have been published. I am also grateful to Julia Bird of Sowelu Associates, Kevin McCathy of Re:Membering Education, Ros Bayley, Heather Jarvis, Toby Greany and Bill Lucas for their comments on the text. The short-comings are all my own.

First Published 2001 by the Campaign for Learning
Campaign for Learning, 19 Buckingham Street, London WC2N 6EF
Reprinted 2002

Printed and bound in Great Britain by Short Run Press, Exeter, Devon.

British Library Cataloguing in Publication Data
A CIP catalogue record for this book is available from the British Library.

ISBN 1-903107-05-9

Produced for the Campaign for Learning by
Southgate Publishers Ltd, The Square, Sandford, Crediton, Devon EX17 4LW.

Contents

Introduction   3

What this book is about   3

Overview   4

Essential elements of a citizenship school   5

Building a new learning constitution: the role of government   6

Part 1: Why citizenship schools?   9

1. What is citizenship education?   11

2. Citizenship and the purpose of education   15

3. The joy and power of learning   26

Part 2: Transforming schools through citizenship   34

4. Creating a culture of citizenship   43

5. Learning freedom: the empowering classroom and curriculum   61

6. Taking part: creating a learning democracy   81

7. Building a new learning constitution: the role of government   99

Part 3: Resources   103

Materials, trainers and organisations for learning citizenship

Ref 6
p 88

This symbol in the main text refers to materials in Part 3

Endnotes   117

About the author   118

Exercises and activities

• What is school for?	7
• Demands and needs of the time	21
• Identifying opportunities for learning	25
• The joy of learning	27
• Power and powerlessness	29
• Developing policy and practice	36
• Writing a school constitution or student charter	44
• Developing shared aims and values	47
• A citizen's welcome	50
• A citizenship approach to home-school agreements	51
• Understanding and resolving conflict	55
• Developing responsibilities	58
• Developing a sense of purpose and personal worth	64
• Sharing responsibilities for learning	68
• Activities for self-assessment and evaluation	80
• Creating a group identity	83
• Transforming nightmares	96
• What I like best about my school	102

Foreword

This book outlines a radical framework for schools in the 21st Century. The Campaign for Learning fully supports the Government's introduction of citizenship into the curriculum as an important first step in developing rounded and socially responsible citizens for the future. But, as Titus Alexander argues so eloquently in these pages, we believe that schools can and must go beyond this to become places where citizenship is experienced as well as taught.

Citizenship Schools shows how embracing citizenship in this wider sense can develop empowered, motivated, successful and fulfilled learners. It may also lead to healthier and more cohesive schools. In part this comes through a recognition of how we learn, but also by showing how schools can genuinely engage with their wider communities. In so doing, they become the hubs of the lifelong learning age.

An initiative-laden school might justifiably ask 'Why should we become a Citizenship School?' Firstly, it is important to note that for many schools the process will not be as difficult as it might at first sound. The examples of current practice in schools that Titus outlines, from circle time to student councils, show how many schools already have many of the pieces of the Citizenship School approach in place. The task now is to draw these pieces together and place citizenship approaches at the heart of their ethos, structure and practice.

The rewards for taking a citizenship approach are potentially enormous. Research has consistently shown that successful schools are founded on a powerful unifying ethos. Furthermore, by engaging parents and the wider community, schools can develop the tremendous untapped resources of family and community learning. And for young people, the motivating prospect of being listened to will develop lifelong and life-wide skills.

Of course, schools will continue to find it difficult to implement the Citizenship Schools approach without support. The current Government's drive to raise standards has provided an important focus on quality and achievement in schools but, as the Campaign has argued in *Schools in the Learning Age,* the time has now come to consider how we can develop a more unified lifelong learning system for the 21st Century. I welcome *Citizenship Schools* as an immensely valuable contribution to that debate.

Bill Lucas
Chief Executive
Campaign for Learning

Introduction

This book is part of a wider discussion about transforming schools to face the challenges of the twenty first century, a discussion taking place in classrooms, schools, education authorities and societies throughout the world.

This introduction outlines its main aims, an overview of the argument and a detailed summary of the essential elements of a citizenship school, as well as a guide to action for local authorities and central government, with an exercise for groups of people to explore 'What is school for?'

What this book is about

This book has three main aims:

1. To help teachers and schools apply the new national curriculum in personal, social, health and citizenship education, from pre-school to secondary, by providing a tool kit of practical ideas.

2. To give policy-makers and practioners an approach to school improvement that is capable of meeting the challenges of a rapidly changing world, by involving all members of the school community, particularly learners.

3. To advocate 'citizenship schools' as the foundations of a democratic learning society.

The concept of 'citizenship school' provides a whole-school approach to bringing the citizenship curriculum alive. It brings together many practical ideas developed by schools to give children, parents and teachers more power in their own lives, such as peer education, circle time, student councils, service learning, peer mediation, philosophy with children, class meetings of parents and much else. These methods enable citizenship to be practised as well as taught.

Unlocking the learning revolution

Above all, citizenship schools aim to give pupils, teachers and parents ways of unlocking the benefits of a triple revolution that challenges learning today:

■ Spectacular growth in knowledge, which makes textbooks and traditional subjects obsolete faster than ever.

■ Dramatic developments in communications technology and knowledge systems through computers, the internet, mobile phones and other innovations which increase access to knowledge and people world wide.

■ Profound discoveries about the brain and learning.

These changes affect the whole of society, not only schools. They will bring about constitutional changes to the way in which decisions are made at all levels, just as the industrial revolution brought about far-reaching reforms in education, society and politics. Industrialisation, mass production and the growth of trade triggered radical constitutional changes based on mass political parties, universal franchise and nation states. The triple learning revolution calls for equally radical changes in the constitution, based on almost universal access to information and ideas. Citizenship schools have the potential to become the local foundations of a new 'learning constitution' for an inclusive society.

Citizenship schools will also help people develop the skills to cope with the aftermath of the twentieth century, in the form of global climate change, multiple environmental crises, population growth, global inequality and mass migration as well as families under stress, social exclusion and changes in the economy.

Exercises and activities

Accompanying the text are exercises for in-service training, pupils and parents, to develop ideas and practices for citizenship. These exercises emphasise the fact that citizenship is about people shaping the society in which they live. Citizenship schools cannot be based on a rigid blueprint, but must be developed by members of the school community working together in a spirit of co-operation, participation and mutual respect.

Overview

This book is both a discussion about the importance of citizenship for improving education and a practical guide to help schools transform themselves into 'citizenship schools', building on current practice and learning from others.

Part One makes the case for citizenship schools. For over forty years, schools have been under increasing pressure. The school system has often lacked the political abilities needed to negotiate a positive relationship between education and society. This relationship has to be based on a new understanding of the purpose of schools as places of learning in a rapidly changing world.

Chapter One defines citizenship, citizenship education and school citizenship, arguing that the emerging recognition of children as citizens and the emphasis on active citizenship are important constitutional changes. It also shows how the concept of citizenship schools relates to a wide range of current government policies on raising attainment, social inclusion, economic development and lifelong learning.

Chapter Two discusses the purposes of school represented by different models of education. It points to the profound tensions in government policy, between an instrumental approach, based on external assessment targets, and an empowerment model based on self-development of people as citizens. It concludes that the government's goals of raising attainment, overcoming social exclusion and increasing economic prosperity can only be achieved by making learning matter for everyone, empowering teachers, involving parents and treating pupils as learning citizens.

Chapter Three argues that learning needs to give people pleasure as well as power over their own lives. Rapid economic change means that people need to value and develop their unique abilities, and also learn how to participate effectively in collective decisions about how the fruits of learning – including science, technology and production - are used. Politics is our collective learning process for managing social change and citizenship is how we take part in it.

Schools are important intermediary bodies between households and the state, with an important role in developing shared values, a sense of community and social cohesion. Going to school should be an apprenticeship in citizenship. More than a subject of study, citizenship is a way of managing our affairs as individuals and as members of society. Learning citizenship is therefore central to Curriculum 2000. If we fully appreciate the importance of citizenship for learning, we will not see schools as education institutions that produce accredited pupils according to targets in a national plan, like a factory, nor as a consumer service for pupils and parents, but as democratic learning communities capable of managing their own affairs and engaging with the world. Citizenship education is ultimately a process through which a school transforms itself into a democratic learning community. If this happens, it will be the start of a constitutional revolution based on the transformation of schools into foundations of a new learning democracy, in which the practice of citizenship in the everyday life of schools is central to the purpose of education.

For learning to matter, it must give people pleasure as well as power over their own lives.

Part Two outlines practical ways in which schools are already becoming 'citizenship schools' and brings them together into a whole-school approach. Chapter Four outlines the school constitution and describes how to create an ethos or culture of citizenship through shared values and responsibilities. Chapter Five outlines ways of empowering pupils through the curriculum and classroom. Chapter Six describes how pupils, staff, parents and the community can take part in decision-making at all levels. Together, these three chapters set out the essential elements of a 'citizenship school'. These are outlined on the next two pages to provide a reference point.

Chapter Seven summarises ways in which local education authorities and central government can support citizenship schools in practice. This is outlined on page 6.

Part Three is a guide to resources to support schools putting these ideas into practice.

Essential elements of a citizenship school

The following summary may be used as a planning guide to create a school in which citizenship is practised as well as taught.

Create a democratic constitution and ethos:

■ Recognise all members of the school community as citizens, with explicit rights and responsibilities, as defined by these elements and the Rights of the Child;

■ Build a shared commitment to democratic vision and values, involving all member of the school community, including staff, students, parents and its local community;

■ Involve all members of the school community in creating fair rules or boundaries;

■ Involve pupils in maintaining peace through peer mediation and conflict resolution;

■ Develop meaningful responsibilities for all pupils such as:
  • managing their own learning, including deciding and planning what to learn;
  • participating in peer education;
  • maintaining the physical environment, within the school and its grounds;
  • communicating through a newsletter, radio, video, website or other media;
  • conflict resolution or mediation;
  • devising and carrying out projects;
  • undertaking research aimed at school improvement;
  • taking part in appointments of teachers, including the head;
  • pupil appraisal and evaluation of teaching;
  • experience of controlling finance.

These responsibilities are intertwined with the curriculum and decision-making.

Create an empowering curriculum which includes:

■ Active development of a sense of self as a person, learner and agent in the world;

■ Equal partnership with parents as a child's first educator;

■ Shared responsibility for learning with pupils;

■ Exploration of values and purpose in all subjects;

■ Emotional literacy;

■ Thinking skills, applied to real as well as hypothetical and historical problems;

■ Learning to learn;

■ Enquiry skills, including listening, writing, researching and discussing;

■ Peer education and mentoring;

■ Skills of participation and action, including negotiating, decision-making and planning;

■ Participating in campaigns or projects for change;

■ Understanding, sustainable development, consumer education and financial literacy;

■ Self-assessment and evaluating the work of others.

An empowering curriculum includes the statutory framework for personal, social and citizenship education.

Develop active participation in decision-making at all levels:

For pupils this means:

■ Learning partners and teams to develop mutual support and confidence;

■ Circle time to develop empathy, relationships and values as well as resolve problems;

■ A pupil council with elected representatives from each class and a meaningful role in all decision-making;

■ Pupil representatives on the governing body;

■ Local and national representation by young people in decision-making;

For parents, participation takes place through:

■ Class meetings (or associations) of all parents of children in each class, meeting two or three times a year to discuss the curriculum, concerns about the class and issues affecting the school, as well as to socialise and support the class;

■ Parents' councils consisting of elected representatives from each class;

■ Parent representatives on the governing body and a whole school council;

■ Parents' representatives on local education committees;

Staff are involved through staff meetings, joint working groups with pupils, parents and community representatives, the governing body and school meeting or council.

For youth and community groups using the school premises, citizenship schools have a community association or council to run facilities and activities.

These levels of participation would give all young people real experience of decision-making and the issues they face in growing up. These would be real decisions, with real consequences, in which young people would have to seek compromise and consensus among themselves as well as with adults.

Community ownership is an eventual aim of a citizenship school. This means that certain legal and financial rights would be vested in the local community, including:

■ legal ownership, in the form of a community trust or charter;
■ community rights to use the facilities by all ages for learning and community cohesion;
■ rights to raise finance through bonds or other prescribed means, as a not-for-profit agency;
■ rights for the whole community to have a say in major changes.

The school is an active community centre, offering access to other services through direct relationships or on site as a 'full service' school, with library, health centre, leisure facilities and other facilities.

These points are developed in more detail in chapters Four to Six.

Building a new learning constitution: the role of government

Local education authorities can support citizenship schools by:
■ identifying, affirming and supporting good practice;
■ helping schools to share experience, ideas and information;
■ co-ordinating policy development and joint projects;
■ organising training;
■ providing a resource centre of materials, information and contacts;
■ developing guidelines and policies;
■ creating learning neighbourhoods, towns and cities;
■ modelling good practice;
■ creating youth parliaments, parents' forums and other forms of participation;
■ providing access to other council departments, statutory services and political processes.

The role of central government
For central government, citizenship schools are a way of involving all members of a school community in school improvement and community development as well as a wide range of national policies for social inclusion, economic development and lifelong learning.

The government can do a great deal to promote citizenship schools:

■ promote the concept of citizenship schools as a model of school self-improvement;
■ provide funds for training and development of school citizenship;
■ sponsor a national network and resource centre to support the development of citizenship schools;
■ offer grants for independent projects which support citizenship in schools, such as peer mediation, service learning, thinking skills, student councils, circle time and other elements outlined in this book;
■ support a national system of recognition or accreditation for citizenship schools, with the prospect of additional funding and freedom, provided certain conditions are sustained;
■ encourage closer relationships between schools and their communities by providing funding for community education use of school premises all year round;
■ create a national youth parliament and encourage the formation of local youth councils;
■ support national organisations of school students and of parents to strengthen their voice in national policy-making;
■ create a national schools forum or commission of parents, young people, teachers and others with an interest in school education to develop and scrutinise education policy proposals;
■ continue to develop the national curriculum as guidelines rather than being prescriptive.

These measures could unleash greater creativity and commitment to learning in schools and their communities. They would encourage schools to make the citizenship curriculum come alive in the everyday life, and give schools a wider role in their local community. Above all, they would enable schools themselves to develop the capacity to respond to the relentless pace of change in knowledge, society and the economy. These points are developed in more detail in Chapter Seven.

The first 16 topics are those set out in the 1997 White Paper, Excellence in Schools. The last four are based on Article 29 of the Convention on the Rights of the Child.

What is school for?

This exercise aims to stimulate discussion about the purpose of school education. It takes 30 to 90 minutes, depending on how much discussion you want.

For a fuller discussion, start by asking each group to discuss the purpose of education, then to rank the different purposes on cards or as a numbered list, before giving out the printed cards below.

Photocopy and cut out the following cards, and create a few blank cards for participants to fill in if they want. Invite participants to form groups of four to seven people. The exercise itself involves the following steps:

1. Ask each group to rank the topics in a priority triangle (put one card at the top, then a row of two, then three, four, five and seven cards at the base), reflecting the actual priorities of the school. Groups must be able to give evidence or an argument for the ranking.

2. Then ask each group to state their own top three priorities, to find out the school's priorities as seen by most participants.

3. Briefly discuss the outcome, particularly any wide differences in views between groups.

4. Repeat the exercise, asking each group to list their ideal priorities. Emphasise that the exercise is about discussing diverse aims of education and coming to an agreement about priorities within each group.

5. Ask each group to share their top three priorities to find out which have most support across all groups.

6. Briefly discuss the outcome, particularly any differences with the first part of the exercise.

7. Allocate each of the top priorities to one or more group and ask each group to list things the school does to promote that priority now and what else it could do to, then report back to the whole group.

For a more challenging exercise, after step 3 ask each group to remove all cards which represent purposes that are dispensable in practice (however desirable they may be). For example, if group members think the school could function without creating fairness and offering opportunities for all, remove these cards. The remaining cards may be low priorities for members of the group, but essential parts of the school's purpose in practice.

▶

Create a society which is dynamic, productive and prosperous	**Offer opportunity for all**
Create fairness for all	**Unlock the treasure that lies within**
Create social cohesion	**Ensure that every child can read, write and add up**
Achieve success across all school subjects	**Provide access to this country's rich and diverse culture**
Develop an understanding of Britain's history and place in the world	**Gain insights into the best that has been thought and said and done**
Learn to respect others and themselves	**Appreciate and understand the moral code on which civilised society is based**
Appreciate the culture and background of others	**Develop strength of character**
Develop attitudes to life and work, such as responsibility, determination, care and generosity	**Become effective citizens of a democratic society**
Develop creativity and skill in the arts	**Challenge inequality and injustice**
Cultivate free spirits	**Learn to learn**
Get a job	**Collective childcare**
Social control	**Promote obedience**
Develop respect for parents	**Develop respect for your cultural identity**
Learn to live responsibly and peacefully in a free society	**Learn to respect the environment**

Part 1: **Why citizenship schools?**

> **Education influences and reflects the values of society, and the kind of society we want to be.**
>
> *Values, aims and purposes of the National Curriculum*

Education expresses our aspirations for the future. Enabling young people to flourish as adults is one of the most important tasks of any society. But what do schools do when the rate of change is so rapid that we do not know what abilities, skills and knowledge will be needed in future? What do they do when they feel under-valued and under pressure?

Schooling under pressure

The demands on teachers are greater than ever. For decades schools have been shaken by reorganisation, inspection, league tables, appraisal, testing, special measures and a barrage of initiatives. The pressure is on to raise attainment for all, to tackle social exclusion and to equip young people for a rapidly changing world. These pressures will not stop. Technology, the global economy, environmental constraints and other changes will transform the world at an accelerating pace.

In 1900 the total amount of knowledge and technology known to humanity was growing at a rate that would double in about 1,500 years. By 1940 the doubling rate was 500 years. By 1990 it had increased to two and a half years and by 1999 it was six months. The sheer pace and scale of change in knowledge – the raw material of the curriculum – means that schools can never stand still.

Almost two decades ago, in The *Challenge for the Comprehensive School,* David Hargreaves wrote 'After the upheavals of the last twenty years many teachers would clearly like a quiet period of consolidation, but most know only too well that this will not be provided. On the contrary, yet more changes are likely to come, and many of these ... will bring yet further problems and burdens for teachers.'[1] As they did.

Hargreaves urged the teaching profession to 'take a stronger initiative in participating in the design of future reform' and 'a more active role in determining the shape of the relationship between education and society'. For this 'teachers will have to acquire a set of skills which the vast majority now lack - political skills.' If they do not, 'the alternative is quite clear: they will continue to be told what to do, the message will be critical and contradictory, and they will be forced back yet further into a defensive and burdensome position.'[2] And so they were.

In terms of political ability, the contrast between public perceptions of health and education are striking. Both services are subject to rapid change in society and technology. In health there are at least as many reasons for politicians to put pressure on the profession as there are in education. Long waiting lists; huge inequalities by area, class and types of patient; and greater competition from private and complementary medicine. But most of the political pressure has been on politicians to provide more money, not on doctors and nurses.

There have been immense political pressures on health services, through reorganisation, changes in funding mechanisms and league tables for different treatments. But public perception and the language of politicians about medicine have been very different from education. The contrast is instructive. We rarely hear about failing hospitals and failing doctors, and when we do, they are described as exceptions and quickly dealt with. Health professions are seen as leading innovation. Research and clinical trials are integral to professional practice. Professional associations are seen to deal with perceived failures by their members. They take public stands on issues such as smoking, diet and boxing. Above all, they are seen as being primarily concerned with people's health. Politically, the health professions have been more adept than education.

What stands out in the politics of health is the active engagement with substance, the health needs of the nation. We can argue about whether the medical model of health is best, but politically the profession has won the argument.

For Hargreaves, the response to constant change was not defensive politics, but the 'difficult task of creating a comprehensive curriculum which meets the full range of needs and talents of all children.' As the pressures on schools continues unabated, the challenge remains.

Schools themselves need to explore fundamental questions about education in order to create robust solutions that can cope with continuous change. Schools cannot expect others, whether education experts, government ministers or local education authorities, to resolve these pressures. By its nature, any external solution is an additional factor to cope with. Therefore schools must engage directly with the changing world around them and devise their own solutions. This means understanding the changing environment and learning from others about ways of responding, creatively and effectively.

Citizenship education is, among other things, about learning how to be effective in public life. If schools are under-funded they have failed to make a political case for proper funding. They have lacked the citizenship skills to convince the public that schools

deserves more of their money. If teachers feel their autonomy has been curtailed, they have failed to convince others about the benefits of autonomy. If schools are under pressure from external initiatives, they have failed to persuade society that they can solve under-achievement, disaffection and other tasks expected of them. If the expectations on schools are misplaced, then schools have not been effective in convincing others of their purpose. In short, schools have not been good at citizenship.

They may have been 'good citizens', in the sense of doing what they are told, but they have not been sufficiently effective in public life to get the funding, support and autonomy needed to stimulate learning. Maybe they don't need or deserve more (and I believe they do), or maybe politicians are out to get them (which I do not believe), but the continuing pressures on schools raises fundamental questions about the ways in schools respond to change and the relationships between school and the rest of society.

Schools throughout the country - and the world - are exploring these same questions and developing different ways of dealing with them. For many, these pressures are a challenge. They recognise the need to answer fundamental questions about education in new ways. Some of the practical solutions they have come up with are described in the second part of this book.

The first three chapters are a more fundamental look at citizenship, education and society. They aim to show why citizenship schools are needed.

Part 1: What is citizenship education?

> **Recognition of the inherent dignity and of the equal and inalienable rights of all members of the human family is the foundation of freedom, justice and peace in the world.**
>
> *Preamble, Universal Declaration of Human Rights*

What is citizenship?

The new national curriculum does much more than add another subject to the school timetable. It promotes a deeper definition of citizenship than exists in law or custom. Although the idea of active citizenship is not new, the citizenship curriculum develops this idea into something that has profound and very positive implications for education and society - if it can be put into practice.

In brief, the citizenship curriculum defines citizenship as the ability to take an active part in public life at all levels, from the school and neighbourhood to the local community, nation and world. It is about belonging, identity, ethics and social responsibility as well as political processes. This deeper definition is important. Traditional definitions of citizenship emphasise duties to the community, society and state, rather than participation, while classical liberal definitions emphasise the formal, legal aspects, rather than the ability to take part. Classical definitions of citizenship are closely concerned with the state as an institution, whereas the national curriculum treats citizenship as membership of society in its broadest sense, embracing the class and school as well as the international community.

By introducing this broader definition through education, schools acquire a very special and important role. As well as offering children skills and knowledge about the world, they aim to provide young people with the ability to actively shape the society in which they live. Schools, in effect, become a leading vehicle for active citizenship.

The Crick Report, on which new curriculum is based, defines citizenship in terms of three intertwined strands - social and moral responsibility, community involvement and political literacy (meaning politics skills, knowledge and values).[3] This definition permeates the national curriculum, but there are ambiguities which must be clarified to identify the essential elements of citizenship.

A deeper definition of citizenship

Children are clearly regarded as citizens, 'actively involved in the life of the school, neighbourhood and wider community' (Programme of Study, KS3). At Key Stage 1 they are still 'preparing to play an active role as citizens' who 'contribute to the life of the class and school' (PoS KS1), but 'They also find out about the main political and social institutions that affect their lives and about their responsibilities, rights and duties as individuals and members of communities' (PoS KS1), which assumes that they are members of society with responsibilities, rights and duties. This effectively treats children as citizens. Although their rights and responsibilities are different from those of adults, as is recognised in the Convention on the Rights of the Child, they are full members of society and as such, junior citizens.

Citizenship is also seen in terms of the ability to take part. Citizenship education is not just about imparting knowledge, but also developing skills and abilities.

There is a strong commitment to inclusive, democratic values throughout the programmes of study, although historically citizenship has been exclusive, often restricted to a minority of the population, and defined in terms of limited legal rights and duties rather than democracy.

The new curriculum places a great deal of emphasis on responsibility, while rights tend to be seen in the abstract, as concepts to be learnt rather than defining features. Every right necessarily creates responsibilities on someone to uphold it, so rights and responsibilities must be treated as distinct but interdependent aspects of citizenship. Rights are a necessary foundation for citizenship, particularly since the Universal Declaration of Human Rights in 1948 and the incorporation of the European Convention on Human Rights into British law from 2000.

One aspect of citizenship not mentioned in the Programmes of Study is accountability, but without mechanisms to hold decision-makers to account, even the most active, knowledgeable and effective citizen can be powerless in the face of arbitrary authority.

Taking part in decisions is in many respects the purpose of citizenship. It is mentioned in the programmes of study, and so should be an explicit part of the definition.

Finally, citizenship exists in relation to a political constitution that defines the structure, rules and forms of public life that govern decision-making at each level (local, national, European or global). Although most nation states have a written constitution, the UK does not, while the constitution of the European Union and global governance consist of international treaties between governments. Most companies and voluntary associations have written constitutions, but most schools and local authorities do not. But all are constituted in ways that define membership, values, rules, rights and responsibilities of citizens.

Elements of citizenship

These considerations lead to a definition of citizenship in terms of nine distinct but interdependent elements:

1. **Membership** is fundamental: the guidelines refer to pupils as members of a class, school community as well as wider communities. But membership does not create

effective citizenship without rights, a sense of personal power and other elements of this definition.

2. **A sense of personal power,** self-esteem and confidence to take part are key features of the PSHE and citizenship curriculum. Without a sense of personal power it is difficult for people to exercise their citizenship except as followers or supporters.

3. **Democratic values,** including freedom, fairness, social justice, respect for democracy and diversity, as mentioned in the programmes of study. Without democratic values citizenship is reduced to consumer sovereignty or loyal servility.

4. **Political and human rights** give legal force to democratic values and protect the freedom for citizens to flourish. These include the UN Convention on the Rights of the Child, which Britain has signed. Schools can also draw up their own Student Charter.

5. **Civic involvement and responsibility** ('active citizenship') is often presented as a central aim of the citizenship curriculum. Rights by definition create obligations on others to uphold them and 'duties to the community' are part of the Universal Declaration of Human Rights (Article 29).

6. **Accountability** is a critical but often overlooked element of citizenship. For schools, accountability mechanisms might include question time in class, student councils or assembly, a complaints procedure and ombudsman, the governing body, external inspection or appeals to the Secretary of State, as set out in many education acts.

7. **The knowledge and skills** 'needed to take an active part in their school, neighbourhood, communities and society', including enquiry, discussion and voting as well as factual knowledge outlined in the programmes of study.

8. **Participation** in democratic decision-making is essential to citizenship in a modern democratic society.

9. **A constitution,** written or unwritten, which consists of the rules that govern the place of citizens in society.

Without any one of these elements, effective citizenship is impaired. However, these nine elements are much broader and deeper than formal, legal or traditional definitions of citizenship. By recognising that citizenship requires confidence, skills, knowledge and values as much as rights and democratic decision-making structures, this definition marks a qualitative shift from both the traditional liberal and the statutory meanings of citizenship.

Legal citizenship consists of nationality (membership of a nation state) and the civic duties and rights which make up the state's constitution, whether written or unwritten. In law, knowledge, skills, values and confidence are all assumed. Ignorance of the law is no defence and everyone is presumed equally competent unless deemed otherwise for reasons of insanity or incapacity. Democratic citizenship means that laws are made by elected representatives of citizens, enforced by an independent judiciary, and that the government is elected. In Britain, decisions are carried out by an independent civil service. No one is above the law and political or administrative decisions are accountable to elected representatives, independent auditors, judicial review, ombudsmen and other mechanisms. Thus democratic legitimacy, accountability, the rule of law and administrative competence are all vital elements of citizenship in law. Active citizenship is a broader political definition which can include community service, public participation and direct action which may at times change or redefine the law.

Legally speaking, children are not citizens and the PSHE guidelines refer to 'their role as future citizens'. But the citizenship curriculum at Key Stages 3 and 4 aims to 'enable them to participate in society as active citizens of our democracy.' This treats children as active citizens and implicitly extends the definition. Thus the citizenship curriculum is also an important political document which develops the meaning of citizenship in practice.

These subtle but significant extensions of citizenship - to include active citizenship and children as citizens - is itself part of the process through which democratic citizenship transforms society. This is a process in which schools could have an increasingly powerful part. By treating young people as citizens and creating democratic learning communities, schools can give future generations a more powerful and positive influence in society than ever before.

It is also significant that this change has come about through education, since education aims to equip people for the future. The world is changing so fast that citizenship cannot be about defending, or taking part in, or even challenging the status quo. Citizenship today is about creating the future.

A 'citizenship school' is one in which these nine elements of citizenship are applied throughout school life, as outlined in part two. The form these elements take could be described as the 'constitution' of the school. A constitution describes the governing principles of an organisation - its aims and values, membership, rules, responsibilities, powers and decision-making bodies. It is the framework for citizenship in practice.

Before we look further at citizenship education, it is worth summarising it as set out in the new national curriculum.

What is citizenship education?

'The school curriculum comprises all learning and other experiences that each school plans for its pupils', according to Curriculum 2000. Young people are learning the whole time as part of the school community and members of society, in and out of class. Citizenship education and personal development are both closely concerned with developing the skills, knowledge and understanding which enable people to become effective members of society, including the school community.

The national curriculum attainment targets for personal, social and health education (PSHE) are:
1. Developing confidence and responsibility and making the most of their abilities
2. Developing a healthy, safer lifestyle
3. Developing good relationships and respecting the differences between people
4. Preparing to play an active role as citizens (at Key Stage 1&2, ages 5 to 11).

For citizenship the attainment targets are:

5. Knowledge and understanding about becoming informed citizens
6. Developing skills of enquiry and communication
7. Developing skills of participation and responsible action

These targets create a definition of citizenship education that can be summarised as 'enabling people to learn and develop the self-confidence, relationships, values, knowledge, understanding and skills to take an active part in public life'.

Citizenship education includes a specific body of knowledge and skills, but it is also an approach to learning, teaching and school life which fosters self-confidence, good relationships, responsible behaviour, enquiry, communication and active participation in the school and community. Unless the whole school ethos and approach fosters these qualities of democratic citizenship, young people are unlikely to develop the specific skills and knowledge required. At its most profound, citizenship education is a process through which a school transforms itself into a democratic learning community.

This book is mainly concerned with developing a whole-school approach to citizenship. Schools have a legal responsibility to teach the programmes of study for citizenship from August 2002. This will be much easier to do if the principles of citizenship education are already present in the life of the school.

Citizenship schools and government policy

Citizenship schools could make an active contribution to many of the government's initiatives, in addition to the citizenship and PSHE curriculum, which might help schools attract additional funding.

These initiatives include:
- School improvement and raising standards;
- The Healthy Schools Initiative to set a national standard and practical guidelines for schools to develop happier, healthier pupils and staff;
- School Plus: Building learning communities to improve the educational chances of young people in disadvantaged areas;
- Sure Start support for parents and children in the early years in disadvantaged areas;
- Connexions support for young people 16-19
- Education Action Zones, which give schools and local education authorities opportunities to experiment with different approaches to schooling;
- New Community Schools in Scotland;
- The Sustainable Development Education Panel and Development Awareness Working Group;
- The work of the National Advisory Group on Creative and Cultural Education;
- Local Strategic Partnerships and the commitment to 'joined up' holistic thinking give schools, local authorities and other agencies incentives to work together in new ways;
- Tackling poverty and social inclusion through community empowerment, family learning, health promotion, economic development and crime prevention.

All these initiatives offer opportunities for funding and support to develop citizenship schools and put some of these ideas into practice. Schools can develop their political skills by putting together proposals, building support and working with other partners to transform their local community through learning, community development and economic regeneration. The School Improvement Fund, Children's Fund, National Lottery/New Opportunities Fund, New Deal, Health Action Zones, Single Regeneration Budget and other initiatives are just a few of the many sources of funding that could be tapped to develop different aspects of citizenship schools.

The concept of citizenship schools gives teachers, staff, parents, pupils and local people a flexible framework capable of responding to government initiatives and other changes in society. In this sense citizenship schools fill a vacuum in the government's programme for constitutional reform, which still lacks a community dimension. So far, constitutional reform has mainly been concerned with devolution, the House of Lords, Bill of Rights, local government and other political measures. The foundations of society, where people live, have hardly been touched. Citizenship schools enable people to create a new learning constitution from the bottom up, within a framework of national and European policies, as well as UN conventions on human rights and an evolving system of global governance.

Part 1: Citizenship and the purpose of education

> **In all actions concerning children, the best interests of the child shall be a primary consideration.**
>
> *Article 3, UN Convention on the Rights of the Child*

What is the point of learning?

When something is not done well, it is often because its purpose is not clear or in conflict with other goals. Many educational reforms by previous governments foundered because they had conflicting aims which were not shared sufficiently by society or schools. The new National Curriculum is an opportunity to resolve the debate about the aims and purpose of schools for a generation or more.

Lack of clarity and agreement about the purpose of schools reflects underlying conflict about what schools are for. This is because the aims of education express aspirations for society, and our society has been so divided it could not create common aims for something so profound as education. The 1997 Labour government is clearer than most, but its policies still straddle conflicting aims rather than resolve them. As a result, its reforms will produce a spurt of development, like the creation of comprehensive schools, the national curriculum, SATs and universal inspection under previous governments, but they will not fulfil the promise of education for the majority, let alone the poor and excluded members of society.

This disappointment can and should be avoided. The conflicts underlying education are too important to duck. Society today is so divided that if we do not decide now what schools are for, it could tear apart. Ministers and their advisers are committed to creating an education system capable of achieving 'a more productive economy, a more cohesive society, a more successful democracy and more fulfilled individuals'.[4] But these aims will not be achieved unless they are properly understood and embedded in the life and purpose of every school. Government can do no more than provide a broad framework and resources. Even the best framework cannot suit the specific needs of every community. Each individual school has to create a learning community capable of responding to the challenges it faces.

If schools were simply institutions of instruction, where people just learnt to read, write and perform essential skills, then perhaps they could be treated as a functional service, measured by their output of literate, numerate persons. But schools are much more than this. They help to shape the character of future generations. What we need is a new model of schooling as citizenship, in which learning gives people power to take part in society, developing their own purposes as free citizens to create a world as it could be.

The aims of state education

In order to clarify our own views, it is worth considering the aims of education as expressed by recent governments. Since 1988 these have been restated three times, first in the Education Reform Act, then in the 1998 White Paper, Excellence in Schools, and most recently in the new national curriculum.

The 1988 Education Reform Act compressed six broad aims into two brief lines:
a) to promote the spiritual, moral, cultural, mental and physical development of pupils at the school and of society; and
b) to prepare pupils for the opportunities, responsibilities and experiences of adult life.

These sound admirable, until you realise they could apply equally to education in ancient

Sparta, medieval England, Nazi Germany or modern Singapore. They say nothing about the values of society nor the adult life for which pupils must prepare. These aims avoid fundamental questions about the society to which education aspires. Their ambiguity hides the deep social divisions in the society for which pupils are preparing. For many pupils, adult life offers few opportunities, while others expect a clear run through university into a profession. To say what kind of society education aspires, to would re-open such divisions and raise questions about whether the means are adequate to the task. It would also bring issues of citizenship into the curriculum, because democracy is (in theory) a fundamental part of the society in which young people are growing up.

Implicit beliefs about schools

What people want from schools expresses their vision of society, which is as diverse as their political or religious views. But the many different views of schooling may be grouped together into three broad streams of belief:

- schools as exclusive communities, based on social standing, common values or conviction, where character, values and group identity often come before content;
- schools as instruments, a means of transmitting skills and knowledge for particular social purposes, which may be economic, technological, spiritual or political and is usually meritocratic in approach;
- inclusive schools, which aim to overcome social divisions through shared education.

In practice, all three strands are woven together in different combinations with other beliefs about education and society. What matters is which strand is dominant. The first strand includes public schools, as well as religious and independent schools, in which affiliation based on class, faith or belief are dominant. The second strand is more functional. It includes the meritocratic, consumer model of education, in which individual choice and opportunity are dominant, as well as some political and economic models which aim to propagate particular skills and knowledge. The third, comprehensive, strand seeks to create an inclusive community that offers equal access to knowledge, skills and opportunities. This strand also includes holistic schools which aim to develop the whole person in a socially inclusive way.

When education was largely a means of equipping people to take their place in society as it was, as rulers, owners, managers, technicians or labourers, a three- or four-tiered system declared its purpose by it structure. Public, grammar, technical and secondary said it all. Learning meant knowing your place and doing your duty or what you were told.

The drive to provide and improve universal schooling is largely instrumental, based on a conviction that everyone needs knowledge and skills to get on in society as it is. Meritocratic instrumental models of education see learning as a means of competing for a place in society. This is still the dominant model among policy-makers, although it means little to people for whom competition is a win-loose game in which the pitch, rules and referee are often against them.

The comprehensive ideal aspires to an inclusive society, in which education aims to create a fairer, more equal society. But it has never had the comprehensive resources nor curriculum needed to achieve it. In many areas comprehensive schools compete with both exclusive and meritocratic schools, thus undermining the comprehensive principle from the start.

Boundaries between these three strands are blurred in practice. Private schools want meritocratic assisted places and some religious schools include people from other faiths, and none. Many independent schools are meritocratic while Steiner and Quaker schools aspire to be inclusive, although the need to charge fees makes this difficult. What matters is the dominant belief which informs policy and action.

At present, the instrumental, meritocratic model is clearly in charge. The government allocates resources and decides a great deal of detail about the curriculum, teaching time, assessment and administration of schools. But the present government also aspires to create an inclusive society in which education helps to create a common core of civic values.

Citizenship schools are a logical development from current policies. They aspire to be inclusive, but aim to combine diversity and social cohesion through an ethos of respect, participation and engagement that enables people to take effective control of their own learning as equal members of society.

Citizenship and the purpose of education

Aims of education since 1997

The 1998 White Paper, Excellence in Schools, is more explicit about the aims of education, and therefore brings the difficult questions about society to the fore. The White Paper set out an ambitious programme for school improvement, listing between ten and sixteen distinct aims in the opening paragraphs.

These claim for education the aim of 'creating a society which is dynamic and productive (aim 1), offering opportunity (2) and fairness for all. (3) Learning can 'unlock the treasure that lies within us all' (4), but its overriding purpose is 'Britain's economic prosperity (1) and social cohesion (5)'. It then spells out the tasks of education in more detail:

■ 'The first task …. is to ensure that every child is taught to read, write and add up'; (6)
■ to achieve 'success across all the other school subjects'; (7)
■ to provide 'access to this country's rich and diverse culture'; (8)
■ to develop an understanding of its history and its place in the world; (9)
■ to 'gain insights into the best that has been thought and said and done'; (10)
■ to 'ensure that children and young people learn to respect for others and for themselves'; (11)
■ to 'appreciate and understand the moral code on which civilised society is based'; (12)
■ to 'appreciate the culture and background of others'; (13)
■ to 'develop strength of character (14) and attitudes to life and work, such as responsibility, determination, care and generosity (15), which will enable them to become citizens of a successful democratic society'. (16)

These are all worthwhile aims, against which progress could be measured. They are a clearer statement of aims than in Curriculum 2000, although they could also be questioned, refined or changed. The priority given to economic prosperity, and to reading, writing and arithmetic as the first task, marks these aims as instrumental rather than empowering. But the White Paper's sixteen aims are part of the rhetorical scaffolding through which legislation is built, and not necessarily enshrined in policy or practice. The reality of the government's aims for education are not

in this preamble, but in the detailed prescriptions defined by assessment targets, league tables, literacy hour, numeracy strategy, Curriculum 2000, performance related pay and inspection. These are mainly instrumental measures which aim to provide all pupils with a solid grounding in basic skills and knowledge, but apart from PSHE and citizenship, they express much narrower aims than the 1998 White Paper.

Aims of Curriculum 2000

The aims and values set out in Curriculum 2000 are even broader than the White Paper, containing over twenty 'values and purposes' and the following two broad aims, which are to be achieved 'in collaboration with families and the local community':

Aim 1: Provide opportunities for all pupils to learn and to achieve. In particular, it should:
1.1 Develop enjoyment of, and commitment to, learning as a means of encouraging and stimulating the best possible progress and the highest attainment for all pupils.
1.2 Build on pupils' strengths, interests and experiences and develop their confidence in their capacity to learn and work independently and collaboratively.
1.3 Equip them with the essential learning skills of literacy, numeracy, and information and communication technology, and promote an enquiring mind and capacity to think rationally.
1.4 Contribute to pupils' sense of identity through knowledge and understanding of the spiritual, moral, social and cultural heritages of Britain's diverse society and of the local, national, European, Commonwealth and global dimensions of their lives.
1.5 Encourage pupils to appreciate human aspirations and achievements in aesthetic, scientific, technological and social fields, and prompt a personal response to a range of experiences and ideas.
1.6 Provide rich and varied contexts for pupils to acquire, develop and apply a broad range of knowledge, understanding and skills.
1.7 Enable pupils to think creatively and critically, to solve problems and to make a difference for the better.
1.8 Give them the opportunity to become creative, innovative, enterprising and capable of leadership to equip them for their future lives as workers and as citizens.

1.9 Develop their physical skills and encourage them to recognise the importance of pursuing a healthy lifestyle and keeping themselves and others safe.

Aim 2: Promote pupils' spiritual, moral, social and cultural development and prepare all pupils for the opportunities, responsibilities and experiences of life.

2.1 Promote pupils' spiritual, moral, social and cultural development.

2.2 Develop principles for distinguishing between right and wrong.

2.2 Develop their knowledge, understanding and appreciation of their own and different beliefs and cultures, and how these influence individuals and societies.

2.3 Pass on enduring values, develop pupils' integrity and autonomy and help them to be responsible and caring citizens capable of contributing to the development of a just society.

2.4 Promote equal opportunities and enable pupils to challenge discrimination and stereotyping.

2.5 Develop their awareness and understanding of, and respect for, the environments in which they live.

2.6 Secure their commitment to sustainable development at a personal, local, national and global level.

2.7 Equip pupils as consumers to make informed judgements and independent decisions and to understand their responsibilities and rights.

2.8 Promote pupils' self-esteem and emotional well-being and help them to form and maintain worthwhile and satisfying relationships, based on respect for themselves and for others, at home, school, work and in the community.

2.9 Develop their ability to relate to others and work for the common good.

2.10 Enable pupils to respond positively to opportunities, challenges and responsibilities, to manage risk and to cope with change and adversity.

2.11 Prepare pupils for the next steps in their education, training and employment.

2.12 Equip them to make informed choices at their school and throughout their lives, enabling them to appreciate the relevance of their own achievements to life and society outside school, including leisure, community engagement and employment.

This statement of values and purposes reminds us that education is a profound human process and that schools play a vital, complex role in society.

These twenty-two aims provide useful guidelines for school education in a democratic society. If you started with these aims, you would create a very different national curriculum from the one being implemented today. This reflects the continuing tension in government policy, between the legacy of traditional schooling and the aspirations to education for empowerment.

In practice, most schools will probably concentrate on the statutory curriculum, particularly those parts which lead to recognised exams against which school performance is assessed. But this statement of aims may encourage schools to develop broader aims for themselves (see exercises on p 44 and 47).

The most significant thing about these aims is that they put personal fulfilment, participation in the world and responsible citizenship at the centre of learning, not curriculum subjects. The curriculum entitlement is clearly a means to these ends, but not itself the end of education. Although, in practice, teachers and inspectors may treat the curriculum as the subject of education, it is only a means to the greater aim of learning and living in an ever-changing world.

If one had to summarise the stated aims of Curriculum 2000, they would be:

To enable every pupil to develop the skills, knowledge, values and understanding for personal-fulfilment as active and responsible citizens in a changing world.

Citizenship and personal development are integral to the whole purpose of education for this government, not just an additional subject alongside others. But it is not yet clear whether the government itself has assimilated the full potential of its own curriculum.

Tensions in government policy

'The curriculum itself cannot remain static,' as the Qualifications and Curriculum Authority (QCA) acknowledges. 'It must be responsive to the changes in society and the economy, and changes in the nature of schooling itself. Teachers, individually and collectively, have to reappraise their teaching in response to the changing needs of their pupils and the ideas and attitudes of society and economic forces. Education only flourishes if it successfully adapts to the demands and needs of the time.'[5]

This highlights an acute tension at the centre of government education policy. The best learning is about people engaging in dialogue, following their curiosity, discovering new things, thinking for themselves and developing competence with words, numbers, books, science, technology and people as they do so. But education is compulsory, the curriculum is laid down by statute, school life is closely supervised by inspection and even teaching methods are increasingly directed from the centre. Politicians, education officials and head teachers anxious about targets bear down on schools, teachers, pupils and parents who appear to be under-performing. The ability of teachers and learners to influence what and how they learn feels heavily constrained.

Schools can narrow opportunities by teaching young people that success comes from following a predetermined curriculum which rewards conformity to prescribed criteria. Rather than responding directly to a changing world, they are taught how to respond to an interpretation of the world mediated by teachers and the curriculum authority. Instead of learning to think creatively and critically, young people learn how to acquiesce, comply with instructions, suppress their own initiative and curiosity. Successful students, teachers and schools do what they are told.

What is worse, the finite world of the curriculum can seem irrelevant to young people's everyday lives. Rather than helping them organise their growing knowledge of the world, it becomes a barrier, inhibiting real understanding and excitement about learning. This is a reminder that a creative teacher and curious students are essential to overcome the inherent limitations of a prescribed curriculum. The best curriculum in the world cannot circumvent the need for good teaching.

As a collective consensus about essential skills and knowledge, a national curriculum

is useful. But there is an inevitable time-lag between changes in society and the curriculum. The amount and range of knowledge is growing exponentially. In less than ten years, the internet and worldwide web have revolutionised access to information and knowledge. Much of our brave new curriculum could be as obsolete as hot metal type or the Morse code within a decade.

If the QCA and ministers have made a mistake about what and how people need to learn for life in the twenty-first century, we will all suffer system failure. Indeed, schooling over the past century has been precisely that: system failure.

Given the pace of change over the past century, it is remarkable how little secondary schools have changed compared with the rest of society. While chalk, slate, candle, gas light, horse and carriage have been replaced by the internet, telephone, electricity, television, computer, car and plane, secondary schools are surprisingly similar to what they were a hundred or more years ago. Primary schools have changed more, but a secondary pupil from 400 years ago would have little difficulty joining a modern class. There are new subjects and some new equipment. The discipline is less overbearing, the teachers more caring. But the fundamental relationships are often similar.

Schools have not changed much because their central purpose remains the same - to provide collective childcare and to transmit discipline, knowledge, skills and values. At an average cost of about £2 an hour, collective childcare is still an important function of state schools, particularly when most parents are wanted in the labour market. But when unskilled work was plentiful, people worried less that many children learned little so long as they did what they were told.

Now that the economy requires greater skills, flexibility and inter-personal abilities, learning is much more important. This means schools have little choice except to change. For the government this has meant, so far, increased pressure on schools to perform. It has also meant quite substantial additional funding for education, often into initiatives other than the mainstream schools budget, as if the government is tentatively exploring alternatives to schooling. But schools will still

have a central role in education, if they can transform themselves.

Making school matter

There is an argument that the growth of educational activities through multimedia, the internet, museums, libraries and other agencies, means that schools themselves will wither. They will certainly diminish if they do not change. In *Learning beyond the classroom,* Tom Bentley, a former adviser to Education Secretary David Blunkett and now director of the influential think-tank DEMOS, makes a powerful case for a system of neighbourhood learning centres for community-based 'learning opportunities and relationships which nurture the talents, interests and needs of every individual learner.' Bentley argues 'that schools will progressively transform themselves to become the hubs of learning networks, centres of learning excellence which aid the development of understanding by brokering learning opportunities with people and organisations in the communities around them.'[6]

Michael Barber, head of the government's Standards and Effectiveness Unit, makes a similar case for 'more systematic and thoughtful' provision for learning out of school and 're-engineering schools' to become champions for individual learners. He argues that the 'welcome shift of emphasis towards school improvement' will not be sufficient to achieve educational success. 'We need to redesign the whole process of learning' to create a learning society.[7]

David Hargreaves, head of the Qualifications and Curriculum Authority (QCA), also advocates the transformation of schools into a mosaic world of institutional fluidity and diversity.[8]

But schools can still have a central role. As Hargreaves argues, schools have a vital role in generating social cohesion and 'some social cement to ensure that people with different moral, religious, and ethical values as well as social, cultural and linguistic traditions can live together with a degree of harmony'.[9] The rationale for the new national curriculum also includes passing on 'the enduring values of society', enabling pupils to 'develop integrity and autonomy and be responsible and caring citizens capable of contributing to the development of a just society'[10] and other social goals. These social goals are also closely connected with the curriculum for personal, social, and health education and citizenship. They give schools and society the ability to respond creatively to constant change. When children are bombarded with information from all directions, school can help them develop a deeper sense of identity, purpose and understanding of the world.

If schools can show that they are capable of meeting the multiple challenges of learning in a changing world, building social cohesion and developing active participation in their local community - as many schools do - they will also be able to make the political case for better funding. Citizenship education is as much about the place of schools in society as about the content of the curriculum. This point is developed in Chapter Four.

Citizenship and the purpose of education

Demands and needs of the time

Education only flourishes if it successfully adapts to the demands and needs of the time.

Qualifications and Curriculum Authority

This exercise aims to explore the demands and needs of the time, now and when children have left school. It is relevant for both primary and secondary schools, as well as adults. It can be done in 45 to 120 minutes, depending on how much discussion you want.

It can be useful to do an exercise like this once a year, in a staff meeting, class meeting of parents, or with pupils in circle time or student council. It can be a useful warm-up exercise before reviewing the School Development Plan or the curriculum. It can also be used in careers lessons.

Preparation: at a minimum, bring 75x100mm cards or Post-Its on which people can write and arrange seating for small groups of between four and eight people round tables, cabaret style, with a flip chart or writing board for the whole group.

For more thorough preparation, produce a 'state of the future' issues sheet and set of topic cards for each table. (See photocopiable materials on p 23). As a prompt for the discussion, write the year when the children involved will be over 30 on the flipchart/board and list key

areas of life, such as: home, families, relationships, food, shopping, entertainment, work/employment, money, neighbourhood, local transport, long distance transport, telecommunications (phone/TV/internet), town/city, region/nation, Europe, world, education post-16, advertising, animals, climate, energy supplies, water supplies, health, genetic engineering, migration, population, space, war (and any other issue you think relevant).

Process: Start by asking adults present to imagine themselves back in the year when they were at school and discuss in pairs what things were common then and what has changed significantly. It may be worth asking each table for one or two points before moving on.

Then ask people to put themselves into the year when the children involved will be 30 or over - write the date on the board or flip chart - and ask each group to write down what they think the world will be like in that year.

The points from each table can then be pooled in a list or an 'issues map' (see below).

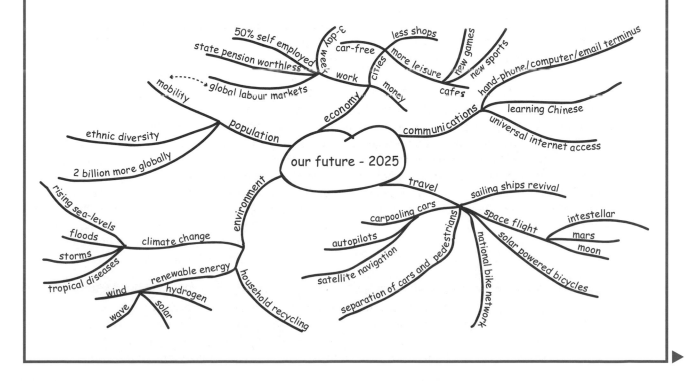

Then ask people to write jobs, skills and knowledge needed for life in that year onto cards (or take the prepared topic cards) and sort the cards into four piles

1) essential for most people
2) desirable for most people
3) needed (i.e. someone will have to perform these skills)
4) not important for most people.

Stress that the aim is to discuss the issues, since right answers are unknowable. For example, self-confidence, writing and reading may appear essential for most people (1), budgeting, goal setting and problem solving may be desirable (2), plumbing and web design may be needed (3) but not necessary for most people to be able to do, and working with cars may be obsolete (4).

Then ask groups to take the cards in piles 1) and 2), and sort them according to whether the main skills, ability or knowledge required for that task are learnt mainly A) at school   B) elsewhere   C) both.

Then ask people to write A, B or C on the cards and put them into a single priority triangle (most important at the top, then two, then three, then five cards, etc). Tasks which need similar skill sets can be put on top of each other.

Ask each group to report on their discussion and the first, second and third rows in the pyramid, noting where the A, B and C topics appear.

Ask each group to compare this list with what children are learning at school. One way of doing this is to take a copy of the school time-table and to note which topics are covered and which are not. Discuss the extent to which young people are learning these things elsewhere, and where.

Finally, ask each group to suggest one change the school could make to help children develop one of the top items that emerged from the exercise.

It is very constructive to compare the conclusion pupils, parents, support staff and teachers might reach as a result of doing this exercise.

Card topics: produce a set of cards for each table, with one skill or area of work on each card. Use the following list, the recruitment pages of local and national newspapers, or the internet to identify as many different skills, needs or demands as possible. (If you are using blank cards or Post-Its, it is worth putting a copy of the list on page 23 on each table to give people ideas).

Citizenship and the purpose of education

Enabling young people to 'respond positively to the opportunities and challenges of the rapidly changing world' is one of the most important tasks of any society. But what do schools do when the rate of change is so rapid that the future is unknown and unknowable?

One response is to redouble our efforts and improve what worked best in the past. The government's emphasis on attainment, school improvement and inspection is largely about bringing all schools to the standards set by the best of what has gone on before. Commitment to excellence and achievement is essential, but excellence in what? Not Latin and classics for all.

Confidence in speaking, reading, writing and number are vital foundations for living and lifelong learning. But attainment will only rise if young people really want to learn what is offered. Even then, high attainment will be irrelevant if they need different skills in the uncharted times beyond school: how much

of today's curriculum will matter in 2020, when some of today's reception classes may start to earn a living? The world has changed enormously since 1985, when some of today's school leavers first started, and the pace of change is accelerating. What if success comes to those who develop distinctive talents during truancy, not the stars of SATs, GCSEs and NVQs? What if today's successful schools, with their well-ordered environments and carefully planned timetables, actually prevent people from making the most of opportunities in the uncertainty of the future? What if the rascals, pranksters and tearaways make the running in 2020, while the dutiful swots who sacrificed their youth at the alter of assessment are redundant, or consigned to routine low-paid brain work at the margins of tomorrow's economy? What if the future rewards creative defiance above obedient achievement? The truth is we cannot know.

Another response to rapid change is to guess what skills and knowledge will be most useful in future, then train people in those skills. Again, the government puts a lot

- accounting
- acting
- administrating
- algebra
- applying number
- architect
- arithmetic
- artificial
    intelligence
- artist
- baby care
- baking
- banking
- bar tending
- beautician
- blacksmithery
- boating
- body guard
- book-keeping
- broker
- budgeting
- building
- business
    planning
- calculating
- camping
- carpentry
- catering
- childcare
- classifying
- cleaning
- clowning
- communicating
- composing music
- cooking/food
- counselling
- counting
- crafts
- dancing
- data

- management
- decision-making
- dentistry
- designing
- drama
- drawing
- driving
- editing
- educating
- electrician
- engineering
- entertaining
- environmental
    work
- estate agent
- exploring
- fashion design
- film making
- fishing
- fitness training
- flexibility
- gardening
- geography
- goal setting
- graphic design
- hairdressing
- health care
- historian
- house painting
- household
    repairs
- improvising
- integrity
- inventing
- librarian
- listening
- lobbying
- magician
- making clothes
- making jewellery

- making music
- manager
- marketing
- marriage
    guidance
- martial arts
- massage
- match making
- mathematics
- mediating
- memory/recall
- mining
- motivating
- negotiating
- nursing
- organising
- painting
- parenting
- peace keeping
- photography
- piloting
- plumbing
- politician
- pollution control
- potting
- printing
- prison guard
- problem solving
- reading
- repairing things
- researching
- self-confidence
- sewing
- shopping
- singing
- social work
- software work
- soldiering
- sound technician
- space travel

- speaking in
    public
- spelling
- spiritual work
- statistics
- survivalist skills
- teaching/training
- team work
- television work
- tool operator
- toy making
- trade union work
- translation/
    languages
- typesetting
- urban planning
- using a joystick
- using a keyboard
- using computers
- visualising
- voice work
- water
    management
- weaving
- web browsing
- web design
- welding
- work in sports
- work with travel
- work with trees
- work with video
- working with
    animals
- working with
    antiques
- working with
    cars
- writing
- writing poetry
- yoga

of emphasis on new technology and key skills, which run through the national curriculum. It also recognises that the arts and specialist skills are becoming more important, although their place in the curriculum is still in question. My guess is the skills for tomorrow are likely to include independence of mind; the ability to form relationships and work with others; solving problems for which there is no right answer, and the bloody-mindedness to persist when everyone else thinks you are wrong. What is certain is that everyone will need to be an effective learner, capable of changing what they do many times during their lives.

A third response is to enable young people to take part in creating their own future. The government's agenda for citizenship is clearly concerned with this.

These three responses to a world of rapid change have radically different implications for how schools are run. They are not wholly exclusive: equipping young people to create their own future requires a grounding in the past, an understanding of problems and possibilities in the present and a capacity for traditional as well as new skills. But the first two approaches assume that an authority (the teacher, QCA or whatever) is capable of laying down what each young person needs to learn for their future. They epitomise a 'teaching society'.

The third approach treats young people as active participants in their own future, authors of their own lives. They are not objects of teaching, who must be made to fit into society, but subjects of their own learning, who contribute to society as citizens of the school and wider community. In this model, the purpose of education, and the future to which it aspires, belongs to every young person in the here and now. But not just young people. As the world changes, so parents, teachers and other adults are also lifelong learners, creating the future. They know from experience that education cannot keep pace with change. We need active collaboration between the hope of youth and insight from experience to thrive in an age of constant change. Where once it was assumed that education always passed from elders to youth, it is increasingly common for children to teach parents

or grand parents how to use the internet, computers, multimedia and other new technologies.

If young people are treated as **citizens,** responsible for their own learning, in a society of lifelong learners, who share responsibility for the school and the world, our whole approach to schools becomes very different.

The government's proposals for education in citizenship and personal, social and health education offer the most productive route to meeting this challenge, but implementing these proposals requires more than additional subject specialists and slots in the time table. They are about changing behaviour and relationships throughout education. If taken seriously, they involve a transformation of schools and their relationship with society.

Citizenship and the curriculum

Many schools see the challenge as how to build citizenship into an over-crowded curriculum when the demands on teachers' time are already excessive. On top of the daily tasks of teaching children and running the institution, teachers have to deal with open enrolment, home-school agreements, league tables, inspection, special needs, the revised national curriculum, increased information technology, the National Grid for Learning, education for sustainable development, changes in funding and a constant stream of initiatives. In this context,

---

squeezing citizenship into the curriculum is not the problem. It is the solution.

The dominant experience of school for most pupils, parents and teachers is one of external control - of being told what to do, conforming to established norms and being told off if one fails. The government sets the curriculum, standards and targets; these are enforced by tests, league tables and inspectors; and implemented through a hierarchy of head, senior staff, class teachers and support staff. People learn their place and are punished if they transgress. This regime is for the good of all - educational achievement is too important to be left to chance. But in the ratio of blame to praise, the noise of accusation drowns out achievement, leaving a lasting sense of guilt, stress and

Citizenship and the purpose of education

dissatisfaction. Good educators know that praise motivates more than fear of punishment.

The school system, from the Secretary of State and Chief Inspector to lunch time supervisors and classroom assistants, is highly prescribed. The dominant ethos is one of direction, control, discipline and, if necessary, punishment by external authorities. Although today's authorities may be more understanding, the penalties for breaching external expectations can be severe. Thus everyone learns to look over their shoulder - child to teacher, teacher to senior staff, school to inspectors, head to local authority, local authority to the government, and government to the media and the electorate. That telling phrase, 'to teach a lesson' means to punish someone for making a mistake, not to share the joy of learning.

In practice, learning today is still about satisfying the prescriptions of external authorities. Although they might have the right prescription for some or even most pupils, this kind of learning is not what people need in a fast changing world. It is the training of subjects, not the education of citizens.

Resolving the tension between personal autonomy and external authority is central for both personal development and citizenship education. The curriculum content may be prescribed, but its practice must be negotiated and increasingly self-determined or it will be a course in hypocrisy. Personal, social and citizenship skills need to be applied to school life as a whole, or they will create unsustainable tensions between a democratic content and a controlling context.

The citizenship solution

The solution is to apply the skills and concepts of personal development and citizenship to the whole school, so that the mainstream curriculum itself becomes enriched in the process. Many teachers are already doing this, particularly in subjects like English, drama, environmental education and design. The challenge is to develop this approach across the whole school.

This means that schools cannot be seen as institutions that produce accredited pupils according to targets in a national plan, like a factory. Schools must become democratic learning communities which manage their own affairs and engage with society as learning organisations.

To do so, they need confidence in their purpose as places of learning. They need to inspire people about learning as a way of bringing about change for the better. This is the subject of the next chapter.

Identifying opportunities for learning

The aim of this exercise is to identify what people in your school community see as the main learning needs and opportunities in their lives. It can be done through questionnaires or as part of a school conference or training session. It is best to get individuals to answer the questions on their own first.

Ask parents, children, teachers and other staff to say what are:

1) the three main benefits of going to school

2) the main skills, knowledge and abilities people need to get on in the world

3) the three most important things that someone needs to learn to have a good life

These three questions can be written on a single sheet of A4 or A5 with plenty of room for answers. They should be anonymous, but answers from parents, children, teachers and other staff should be identified separately, by different coloured paper and a letter or word. Parents and children from different years could be identified by asking what year they or their children are in. The responses should make interesting and useful reading.

Part 1: **The joy and power of learning**

> ## This requires from political leaders a playful attitude.
>
> *David Hargreaves, on the evolution of schools for the future*

Play is a child's work. It is how the young of the species learns. Play is also central to the human spirit and learning. Mature play is highly disciplined, like sport, music and other arts. Casual play, like conversation, day-dreaming, pub games or gossip, is the glue of everyday life. The essence of play is that it is freely undertaken, in free time, a leisure activity when the necessities of life are looked after. Greek philosophers believed that we become most fully human in free time devoted to self-development. Thus the Greek word for leisure, *scholea*, gave us 'school'. The Latin *Ludus* means both play and school.

Leisure and the ability to do what you want are touchstones of human freedom. People's aspirations to win the lottery, buy or invent labour-saving devices, to go on holiday and have fun are all ideals of freedom. Civil liberties means the freedom to believe, say and do whatever you want, so long as it does not infringe the liberties of others. Economic freedom includes freedom from want and the ability to produce or have what you want, provided it does not harm others or the environment. These freedoms are the true aspirations of education.

Freedom is only possible when people have the power to exercise it. This includes inner confidence as much as external circumstances. Democratic citizenship in ancient Athens as well as modern Britain was developed by minorities who had the free time and self-confidence to participate. Today everyone has the right to take part in government, but in practice most do not have the freedom to do so, because they lack the skills, knowledge or confidence to do so.

People's devotion to sports, hobbies, amateur arts, pub games and the creativity of our comedy, pop music and television demonstrates a large and lively culture which appears only at the margins of school, as unofficial, extra-curricular activities. But it is often these activities which give young people the confidence, skills and even opportunities in later life. Those who only stick by their books are often diminished by them. And let us not forget that the enjoyment of reading, writing, maths and even science were often leisure activities in origin, pursued for their own sake more than practical application. Many of our societies' greatest achievements were created in defiance of authority and the accepted teaching of the time.

Real learning may be hard work, but it is also a joy. Love of learning spurs people to continue learning throughout life. Creativity, invention, discovery and development come from the joy of learning, not duty or even necessity. Indeed, when everyday necessities become a source of joy, like cooking and eating, people take part with pleasure. What is toil to some, like gardening, house painting, making clothes, DIY, driving or catering, are leisure pursuits for many. One sign of real success in life is to be paid for what you love doing. And the sign of a successful society is when everyone loves what they do.

The joy of learning is also fuelled by a sense of purpose, because human beings are a purposeful species. We conceive possibilities in our imagination, then strive to realise them. We follow our goals to create, make, mate, buy, save, invent and do all kinds of things. People with a sense of purpose work hard to learn and do whatever it takes to achieve what they want. Unfortunately many people do not feel they have the freedom to do want they want, and many do not know what they want because they have been taught only to aspire to goals set by others.

This highlights a tragic paradox of our age: humanity has the talents and productive capacity to create a world in which everyone has enough, with an abundance of free time, yet many people work harder and longer than ever, suffering from stress, while others are unemployed or toiling without satisfaction.

The joy of learning

This short sentence completion exercise aims to stimulate thinking about what is really important to people. It can be done by teachers, support staff, pupils or parents, seated in a circle or in small groups. It takes 5-15 minutes and can be used to encourage people to connect their personal aspirations with their work. The exercise can be done in pairs if people might be uncomfortable about sharing personal aspirations in a group.

Before starting it is worth agreeing a few ground rules, such as:

● **confidentiality:** anything said will not be repeated elsewhere;

● **non-judgmental:** listen without comment or judgment on what people say.

The person leading the exercise reads out a sentence stem from the list below and asks people to completes the sentence in turns. It is best to start by reading a sentence stem, then giving people a few minutes thinking time. The leader completes the sentence themselves to start with, giving their honest response, then asks who would like to go next. It is not necessary to go strictly round the circle. You can do as many or as few sentences as you want, and each sentence stem can be done several times.

"I experience most joy when I ..."

"I am happiest when I ... "

"If I could do anything I wanted, I would ... "

"If I knew I could not fail, I would ... "

"If I had three wishes, I would ... "

"If I won £10 million in the lottery, I would ... "

This exercise can be the starting point for a discussion of purpose, life-goals or careers.

The playful economy

Leisure is already a major part of the economy and the largest item of household expenditure.[11] Most families spend between a sixth and a third of their income on leisure, on average 23 per cent including smoking and drinking. Eating out, the arts, entertainment, film, gardening, music, sports, tourism and other leisure activities are a large part of national income and employment. To this we should add a large part of fashion, domestic consumption, car ownership, computers and other items enjoyed for pleasure rather than necessity. The creative sector alone has been valued at over £60bn. Creative services are a fast growing export sector, with income from film and television exports increasing by 7 per cent a year. Since 1970, services have expanded four times faster than manufacturing. On average, about half of waking time (54 hours a week) is occupied with leisure activities at home, of which almost half is spent in front of the television or video. With the age of retirement often below 60 and life expectancy still rising,

most people in Britain today can expect to spend most of their lives in leisure activities.

The shift in free time is truly dramatic. In 1856, the average full-time working week was 65 hours. By 2000 average working hours had almost halved, to 35 hours a week (i). Average annual working hours fell from 3185 hours a year to under 1700 hours. A century ago, most people worked over half of their adult life time (excluding 10 hours a day for eating and sleeping). Many started work at 13 or 14, sometimes younger, and toiled until they died, usually before 60. Today, the average adult has three times as much free time, over 80% of their lives. Total free time has grown from about 118,000 to over 287,000 hours (see

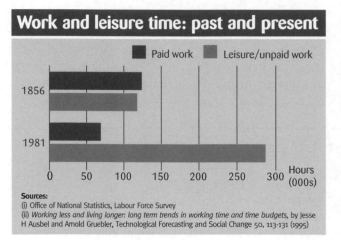

Work and leisure time: past and present

■ Paid work   ■ Leisure/unpaid work

1856

1981

0   50   100   150   200   250   300   Hours (000s)

Sources:
(i) Office of National Statistics, Labour Force Survey
(ii) *Working less and living longer: long term trends in working time and time budgets*, by Jesse H Ausbel and Arnold Gruebler, Technological Forecasting and Social Change 50, 113-131 (1995)

graph), with the crossover from a majority of work to non-work as early as 1900 (ii).

These statistics reflect a profound shift in the purpose of life for the majority of people, from toil to pleasure and the fulfilment of human potential. But our beliefs, culture and political economy have not caught up with this transformation. The economy is still driven by relentless pressures. In many jobs people work harder than ever. Those on low incomes earn too little to enjoy this increased wealth in time and the unemployed are often unable to enjoy their enforced leisure. These issues are beyond the scope of this book, except to observe that a relatively high proportion of most people's income today is spent on mortgage debt and other financial services.

The world is changing in ways that increase the importance of education for freedom rather than economic servitude, because the economy itself is more diverse and open to individual initiative than ever before.

It is therefore a human tragedy that learning is treated as an instrument of industry, a necessary chore rather than a priceless pleasure. The cost of this tragedy is low attainment by those whose spirits are crushed. This is not a sudden tragedy, but deeply rooted in the culture of employment, education and society that goes back a century or more. Many schools and teachers inspire a love of learning in their students. The question is, why is this not the norm?

In my view this is because those responsible - the politicians and officials in national and local government - treat education as an instrument, a functional service for society and the economy, not as a profound human

process. They treat schools like factories, where outputs are measured by statistics and inspection, not by the quality of life they create. And they treat teachers as functionaries, who carry out national plans to meet prescribed targets, not as capable human beings who inspire learning if they themselves are inspired.

The concerns of politicians and employers about attainment in education are justified, but achievement without a sense of joy, power and purpose is pointless. We will not create a learning society until the joy of learning is kindled in every child, then fanned and fuelled throughout life. This means empowering teachers and schools to enable people to define and fulfil their own purposes in life. Of course this includes mastery of words, numbers, information technology and knowledge. But it also includes learning to learn, inquire, question, solve problems, take responsibility and develop social values. Above all, it requires a passion for learning and for life.

The power of learning (and learning about power)

Learning changes the world. Science, technology and social invention create ceaseless change. Learning transforms production, employment and society. Learning enables people to exchange ideas, information, money, services and goods faster than ever before. Learning can create opportunities and greater earning power. Learning also enriches people culturally and socially. Learning is powerful.

But those who are not part of the learning revolution get left behind. They are excluded and increasingly marginalised. Constant change demands new skills and new ways of doing things. While learning liberates some people, it makes others redundant. The fast moving global economy wipes out crops, cultures, habitats, industries, languages and species, as well as spreading diseases like aids, malaria and tuberculosis. The conquest of America created a continent of discovery for Europeans, but was an utter disaster for the native peoples. Industrial change can bring benefits for some but have devastating consequences for others. What is scientifically possible may not always be desirable, as the tragic experience of tobacco, asbestos, thalidomide, BSE, global climate change and other innovations teach us.

Power and powerlessness

Power, n., Ability to do or act; government, influence, authority (over); force; from the Latin, posse, to be able

Shorter Oxford Dictionary

This discussion exercise aims to explore experiences of power and powerlessness in school. Parts One and Two together take 30 - 90 minutes, depending how much discussion you want. Part Three can take the same again and can be used to lead into a discussion of citizenship schools. This exercise can be developed in various ways, some of which are suggested below. It may be useful to display dictionary definitions and quotes about power for reference and stimulus.

This exercise can be done with groups of teachers, governors, parents, pupils or members of the community. When doing it with a mixed group, it is worth starting with separate groups for teachers, governors, parents or pupils, then letting each group share their experiences. The second and third parts of the exercise can be done in separate or mixed groups. It can be very useful to ask small groups to share the main points from their discussion after each step of the exercise.

Part One is about defining power. Divide into pairs or groups of five to seven people. Ask each pair group to discuss briefly what power means to them and write the main points on a flip chart.

Part Two is about sharing experiences of power and powerlessness. Ask people to form pairs and take turns to describe an experience, without interruption, of powerlessness in school, as pupils, parents or in any other role. This can be a cathartic exercise for some people, so be sensitive and supportive.

Pool experiences from the group, taking different roles in turn, starting with experiences as pupils, then as parents, then as support staff, teachers, managers, governors and other roles in turn. List key words on a flip chart.

Then ask pairs to share experiences of power in school - times when they felt able to act, to influence what happened and to be in control of what they did. For each experience, ask the group to write a word or two about what contributed to that sense of power.

This exercise can be continued by asking each group to briefly list:
● the negative consequences of a sense of powerless by different groups in school (be specific about the consequences for pupils, parents, teachers, governors and others feeling powerless);
● the benefits of enabling different groups to be more powerful (again, be specific);
● the challenges that can arise when different groups become more powerful.

The challenges of empowering different groups can create anxiety or even fear and a greater sense of powerlessness among other groups in school, so it is important to address these fears, to acknowledge the negative consequences of powerlessness and recognise the benefits.

Conclude Part Two by asking each group to identify two or three steps to increase a sense of power in school. These points can be used for the following activity.

Part Three is about fostering a sense of power in school. Ask pairs or groups to identify ways of encouraging a greater sense of power within school. This can be done in the same groups as Parts One and Two, with each group building on the previous discussion, but it can be more useful to form new groups round topics arising from the discussion, such as: teaching and classroom practice; induction (of new pupils, parents and staff, separately); work with parents; pupil responsibilities; behaviour, rules and discipline; decision-making; community service.

For each suggestion, participants should be asked to say something about:
1) the current situation;
2) benefits of change;
3) specific actions, routines, rules or physical changes required;
4) possible obstacles and what to do about them;
5) preconditions and support required;
6) when, how and by whom changes could be made.

It is not enough that people are educated so that British firms compete successfully in the global knowledge economy if as a result:

- some people are excluded or drawn into the illegal economy of drugs and crime;
- society becomes increasingly fragmented and unstable;
- new technologies cause environmental or social damage; or
- the world becomes more polarised and dangerous.

Education is also about developing the ethical, cultural, political and social understanding that makes life worthwhile. Education must also enable people to thrive despite changes in industry, employment and the environment. Learning advanced skills and knowledge may be worthless without the wisdom to reflect on how they are used and the ability to de-cide collectively, as a society, how the fruits of science, technology and the economy are used. Politics is our collective learning process. Learning how to use power is there-fore an essential dimension of education.

Political processes are often more important for our personal potential than individual learning. Some social arrangements clearly increase individual opportunities for fulfil-ment, while others stunt them. The stark contrasts between North and South Korea, East and West Berlin before 1989, Uttar Pradesh and Kerala, Myanmar (Burma) and Singapore, Tallin and Helsinki on opposites banks of the Gulf of Finland, or Soweto and Santon in South Africa, dramatically illustrate the difference that social and political arrangements make to individual opportunity.

Likewise, school systems and social context can make more difference than the efforts of individual students, teachers or parents. On their own, everyone may work incredibly hard. But poor opportunities, lack of support and adverse circumstances can work against them. A bright, hard working child in a well-run state school in a deprived neighbourhood with many disturbed, difficult children, may do less well academically than a slower child from a privileged background in a private school with 16 well-behaved children in each class. But the more diverse social milieu can give pupils opportunities to develop a much wider range of skills and insights.

It is not enough to say to someone, learn and you will increase your life chances. The learner needs to know that they have the power to apply their learning and to benefit from it. And if they do not like the conditions under which they live, they need the power to take part in the collective learning process of society, through politics as well as markets.

Raising school standards without empowering all learners could increase social exclusion, because it leaves behind those who do not appreciate the power of learning or lack the circumstances to make learning matter.

Making learning matter

If we can kindle and sustain the excitement of learning in every parent and child, they will be the driving force for attainment, and they will seek out the skills and knowledge which give them an active role in shaping the world. Teachers, schools, education advisers, authorities, inspectors and ministers can do

much to inspire or to stifle learning. But the spark of learning must burn within each child and the adults who matter in their lives.

To kindle the spark, every parent and child must know that they matter as much as learning. Learning skills set by distant powers can make the desire to learn equally distant. It is no good training people to chase jobs that are changing faster than the curriculum. In a community where the steel mill is replaced by a silicon chip factory, which is succeeded by call centres that will be supplanted by internet web sites, people may learn that schooling matters little.

For learning to matter, it must have real power in people's lives, not just at the end of an 11- or 16- year long time tunnel. Learning has to matter in the process of learning itself. This includes a sense of satisfaction through achievement. It also includes a sense of ownership - learning for oneself, not just for Miss or Sir, for Ofsted or a national target. It includes a sense of competence that qualifies one for whatever opportunities may arise in future, and also the capacity to create opportunities. It includes a facility with ideas, words and number, but also the power to seek out and shape ideas or words that matter to you. It includes the respect that comes from following rules, and the power to change the rules through a political process. And it means that learning serves the community in which you are growing up, not just employers who come and go. Above all, it means learning with joy, as a free person, able to choose how to use your time.

This is about learning as citizenship, not just a consumer good provided by a choice of schools. The paradox is, the joy of learning is also at the heart of the new global economy.

An economy based on knowledge, information and services can only function if people are flexible, skilful and above all capable of thinking for themselves. Enjoyment and learning at work are vital for sustained productivity. Employers know they have to treat people with respect or lose business. In many areas, authoritarian management simply does not work. Leading industries invest in people through staff development and support because their survival depends on it. Business now spends a third more than the government on education and training. A growing number of employers also recognise that a divided, unequal and unjust society is bad for business as well as society.

But business cannot create social cohesion. That comes from the way in which we live together, as households, neighbourhoods, towns and nations. Schools, more than any other universal institution, have the potential to build social cohesion at a local level.

Consumer service or crucible of citizenship?

Schools are not just instruments of instruction or information channels. Skills and knowledge could be delivered more efficiently and attractively in other ways. The core curriculum of reading, writing and arithmetic can be taught in about a hundred hours to pupils eager to learn. The entire curriculum and more is available on the internet for those who want to study at home. But the vital, irreducible quality of schools is in the understanding, values and relationships among its members. Living in society requires shared ethics. These can only be developed through human relationships.

Schooling is more than a consumer good. Like choosing a partner, following a faith, joining a profession or acquiring citizenship, attending school demands commitment. It means joining a community which requires certain attitudes, ways of behaving and values. But pupils have few rights and many duties. Sanctions for breaking them are fairly explicit and most pupils learn to comply, even if only by adopting a temporary mask during school hours. The culture and ethos of a school still mean more than the content of lessons.

Going to school is an apprenticeship in citizenship. Just as families and states seek to balance freedom and responsibility within their boundaries, so school communities regulate their own affairs as microcosms of society. Like families or states, schools can be authoritarian, oppressive, democratic or progressive. This small 'p' political culture of schools needs to be explicit if young people are to develop the practice of citizenship and power of learning.

Every society needs intermediate social units between families and the nation. Unlike shops or cities, families and nation-states both re-quire reciprocal obligations based on need and ability to contribute, rather than on commercial exchange. Today most intermediate social institutions have shrivelled in importance or disappeared, leaving society more fragmented and divided. In many areas there are no organisations which bring people together at a local level, except exclusive clubs and gangs. Most other institutions, from markets to local government, have impersonal relationships with people and involve little mutual commitment.

Schools are often the only institutions in which a substantial part of the community is linked in any meaningful way. Many schools bring together people from different faiths, denominations, social backgrounds and ethnic origins. This makes schools natural successors to places of worship as a focus for community life, in which community values, experience and knowledge are shared and developed.

The development of schools as the building blocks of local communities, linking families in a common endeavour, should be seen as a crucial branch of constitutional reform, more important than devolution, proportional representation or our relationship with Europe.

Schools create social value

Every school shapes, and is shaped by, the emotions, imaginations and values of its members. All schools seek to transmit what they see as most essential to be passed on to the next generation. Each one is, in its own way, an active expression of a vision of the world in which young people are growing up, including their history and future. This vision may be barren or rich, functional or multifaceted, closed or open, confused or orderly. Whatever it is, this vision influences the attitudes, behaviour and values of people who pass through school. As Einstein said, education is what is left after you have forgotten everything you learnt.

Good schools enable people to transform their lives. Young people discover and develop themselves by learning together with experienced adults. They form a sense of identity and purpose that equips them to face life's challenges. Parents often become more interested in learning themselves when their children go to school. Some parents become active in the local community through school,

organising after-school activities, helping at school events or campaigning. A local school that becomes a centre of attraction with a high standard of learning can transform the fortunes of an area and its people.

These are all vital aspects of learning that may not appear in the curriculum and cannot be tested in exams, but may be more influential than examination scores. At present, this quality of experience is probably more common in schools that cater for an exclusive community, such as religious, independent or public schools, but many comprehensive and community schools also achieve these qualities. It is not surprising that schools which have clear values and a positive ethos achieve better exam results than those which do not, given pupils from similar backgrounds.

But the experience of citizenship is much rarer. Citizenship involves a real sense of your own power as a person, with the ability and conviction that you can shape your own destiny as an equal. Public schools do this for an exclusive community. But learning in a democratic society must give everyone that sense of power over their own lives as truly equal citizens.

Learning citizenship

The ethos, organisation, structures and daily practices of schools, including whole-school activities and assemblies, have a significant impact on the effectiveness of citizenship education.
Crick Report, 1998[12]

Citizenship is learnt above all through experience, by taking part in activities, discussion and decisions which have a real influence on what happens. Citizenship education that takes place in an environment that learners cannot influence is more likely to lead to cynicism and an even greater sense of powerlessness. Charles Handy has compared schools with city states,[13] but most pupils, parents and even teachers do not feel like citizens. Pupils have relatively little responsibility, except to do what they are told and fulfil expectations set by others. Teachers have a great deal of responsibility, but often feel they have little control over what they do. If citizenship education is to mean anything, then it must start with pupils taking real responsibility for the environment, management and learning in school.

Schools are ideal institutions in which to learn citizenship in practice. They are relatively self-contained, with a well-defined local membership, relatively clear decision-making structures, and an elected governing body representing most stakeholders apart from pupils. Schools now manage their own budget, staff and relationships with other agencies, subject to external inspection, the local authority and national directives.

Learning citizenship in practice means developing the skills of listening, understanding other people and issues, building trust, winning and losing arguments, coming to agreement, communicating, establishing effective relationships and, above all, being responsible for making decisions which have real influence in the world, for which we are accountable. These are essential skills in a constantly changing, uncertain world.

The underlying argument of this book is that improving education and tackling social exclusion also means transforming schools into democratic institutions. Democratic renewal from the bottom up is part of the learning revolution needed to take full advantage of the new technologies and a knowledge-based economy. This means that the economic and political landscape itself will change, as more people participate in public life at a local level. Like the constitutional reforms which created the Scottish and Welsh parliaments, or abolished hereditary peers, this will have far-reaching consequences. Unlike them, the democratic reform of schools could enhance the lives of more ordinary people than any overtly political revolution.

Conclusion to Part One

Education of the child shall be directed to the preparation for responsible life in a free society which respects others and the environment.
Article 29, UN Convention on the Rights of the Child

For decades schools have been under pressures to meet conflicting social goals. Education reforms have been imposed on schools because, in part, they lacked the political abilities to respond to changing needs and circumstances. Citizenship skills are required

by schools as well as pupils to secure their place in a rapidly changing world.

Education reflects the aspirations of society. British society is deeply divided, and this is reflected in disparities between privileged private schools and struggling comprehensives on sink estates. Until recently, national education policy had no explicit educational or social aims. But for the first time, the national curriculum sets out a clear vision for education and society. Citizenship education is central to the new curriculum, but there is a tension between externally driven reforms based on an instrumental model of education and citizenship as a democratic process. But resolving the conflict between external authority and self-determination is itself part of citizenship education, so 'citizenship schools' are a way in which these tensions at the heart of the curriculum can be tackled at a school level.

Education is too complex to offer simple solutions to the many difficulties faced by schools. Schools need to devise their own solutions to the pressures on them, by actively involving pupils, parents and staff as 'learning citizens' of the school community. Learning citizenship is not an optional extra. It is fundamental to the success of every student and our society in a fast changing world.

Knowledge, skills and understanding are a vital part of overcoming social exclusion, individually and collectively. But people have to see the relevance and potential of learning. Where education is founded on fear, natural curiosity is stunted. Where the curriculum is seen as irrelevant, young minds wander.

So long as people do not have the ability and power to direct their own affairs, they will be subject to the decisions of others and dependent on others to transform their circumstances. People who are deprived and socially excluded have the most to gain from changing their circumstances. They know best what they need, but lack the means to make it happen. Effective citizenship is therefore an essential part of the process through which people create opportunities to improve their own lives and community.

The next section offers practical ways of creating a citizenship school.

Part 2: Transforming schools through citizenship

> **Children should be 'fully prepared to live an individual life in society and brought up in the spirit of the ideals proclaimed in the Charter of the United Nations and in particular the spirit of peace, dignity, tolerance, freedom, equality and solidarity.'**
>
> *Preamble, The UN Convention on the Rights of the Child*

Bringing citizenship to life

Most people experience citizenship as a sense of powerlessness in the face of events beyond their control. As a result, citizenship is often expressed as apathy, boredom or frustration. At school, the experience of citizenship - the sense of taking part and influencing events - is rare. But it is also fundamental to learning and achievement in a fast changing world.

There is a great deal of evidence that a school's ethos, its 'agreed ways of doing things', has a powerful impact on learning and teaching. Research shows that pupils achieve more if the 'agreed ways of doing things' include high expectations, shared purpose, teaching that is intellectually challenging, frequent praise and feedback, effective discipline, giving children responsibility and parental involvement. The agreed ways of doing things must also be consistent throughout the school and have the general support of all staff.[14]

The 'agreed ways of doing things' could be described as the school's constitution. It includes the many different relationships, practices, rights and responsibilities that define how a school works. Like the British constitution, it is not written down in a single document, but defined by custom and practice as well as specific policies.

In the twenty first century, it is not enough to have a consistent ethos among the staff who manage pupils. From an early age, children are used to having choices. Television and computer games have taught them to expect high levels of stimulation from competing attractions. Mentally, they live in a fast-paced, action-packed, often glamorous world. If the school's ethos is to have an impact, pupils themselves must be part of the process of creating and sustaining it. This is the essence of school citizenship.

> *Personal, social and health and citizenship contribute to the school curriculum by helping to give pupils the skills, knowledge and understanding to lead confident, healthy, independent lives and to become informed, active and responsible citizens. Pupils are encouraged to take part in a wide range of activities and experiences across and beyond the curriculum, contributing fully to the life of their school and communities. In doing so they learn to recognise their own worth, work well with others and become increasingly responsible for their own learning.*
>
> **Framework for PSHE and Citizenship at Key Stages 1-4**

Citizenship comes alive in specific moments when people take part in shaping events, such as campaigns, elections, committee meetings, demonstrations or involvement in a community project. On an historic scale, citizenship moments include constitutional change or revolutions, when systems of government changed. The defining elements of citizenship are a sense of belonging, shared responsibility, involvement and power to make things happen in association with others, as well as the protection and rights society gives its members.

In a citizenship school, a sense of involvement is the norm. For children, choosing a school, starting school, taking responsibility for something, planning lessons, speaking in class, taking part in peer mediation, standing for election to a student council or governing body, participating in decisions and speaking in assembly are all decisive experiences of school citizenship. For parents, the home-school agreement, parents' evening and class meetings could be a potent experience of citizenship, although in practice they are often boring and frustrating. Staff may experience school citizenship when taking part in a working group that brings about change, when being interviewed for appointment by pupils, receiving a pupil appraisal or discussing the school development plan with the student council.

The challenge is to give all pupils, parents and staff a sense of power to create a world of learning that works.

A central aim of education in citizenship and personal development is to enable pupils 'to become more self-confident and responsible in and beyond the classroom'. Responsibility develops through practice, as members of the school community exercise real responsibility for school life. At present, responsibilities of children and parents are often limited to doing what they are told. In most schools, children spend hours following instructions, waiting or standing in line. Even learning citizenship can be a chore if children do not feel empowered. As an eight year-old said recently, "It's so boring when they keep telling you that making the world a better place means picking up litter and not killing whales."[16]

A starting point for planning the citizenship curriculum itself is for teachers to identify what experiences and inputs young people need to meet the citizenship curriculum and then to consider where, when and how they can be developed. This will include existing subjects as well as activities like student councils and citizenship lessons. Many specific topics within the citizenship curriculum need specialist input, some of which can be supported by outside speakers like local

Highfield Junior School

Highfield Junior School in Plymouth is transforming itself into a citizenship school. It is in many respects a typical school in a poor area with few opportunities. This transformation is described in a remarkable book[15] full of practical details and illustrations, produced by members of the school. At its centre is circle time, a forum for each class to build self-esteem, agree rules and sort out problems. Representatives from each class form a School's Council, which meets every two weeks. Conflicts between pupils are sorted out by peer mediation, 'bully busters' and 'guardian angels'. Children are also involved in the appointment of new teachers, induction weeks and a wide range of other responsibilities.

councillors, MPs, lawyers or business people, or visits. As far as possible, pupils and parents should also be involved in planning the citizenship curriculum. The grid on page 38 provides a tool for whole-school planning as well as for subject teachers and departments to identify where and how citizenship can be developed across the whole curriculum.

But simply mapping citizenship topics onto the curriculum misses the point. Citizenship is an active process of developing responsibility, which affects every aspect of school life. It means teachers and other staff sharing control with other members of the community, particularly pupils. In a citizenship school, responsibilities are shared in

Developing policy and practice

There are many different ways of introducing the ideas in this book to your school, depending on your position and other factors. The following nine point process suggests a sequence of steps which should ensure that ideas are properly considered and have sufficient support to be carried out successfully.

As far as possible, ideas should be considered in relation to the school development plan, within its planning cycle, to avoid overloading people with initiatives. But wherever an idea starts, it is worth following these steps:

1. Raising and identifying the issue
Make people aware of the idea you want to introduce, or the problem you want to address together with the possibility of doing something about it, and bring it to the appropriate forum (circle time, class meeting, student council, governing body, etc).

2. Gain consent for something to be done
Unless the idea is relatively small and easy to introduce, it is best to get agreement in principle first and then involve all relevant sections of the school community in developing the details of how it will work in practice.

3. Defining and delegating the task
A small working group should have overall responsibility for seeing the process through. It may be delegated by the governors, staff meeting, senior management team, head teacher, student council or school assembly. The composition of the group will depend on the task, but involvement of pupils, parents or governors should be encouraged where possible. Task groups should have clear terms of reference, a deadline and support from senior management.

4. Audit or investigation
 Depending on the size of the task, commission an individual or working group to do an audit of current policy and practice. This might look at:
● national and local laws or guidelines;
● examples of practice in other schools or organisations which could provide lessons;

● relevant school policies;
● current practice within the school, or another school: many of the ideas outlined in this book are already taking place in many schools on a small scale or in embryonic form, so it is worth learning from and building on current practice.

Student investigations are another way of addressing this stage

5. Preparing a proposal for consultation
The working group produces a proposal for consultation, which may be in the form of a paper, picture or other medium, whatever works and can be understood by everyone who might be affected by it. This may be a proposal in principle, in which case more detailed work has to be done after it is agreed, or a detailed proposal.

6. Consultation
The proposal is presented to all relevant groups, discussed and responses compiled.

7. Decision-making
The relevant body decides on the proposal and who is responsible for carrying it out.

8. Monitoring
Implementation is monitored, to see how it is working in practice and changes made if necessary

9. Evaluation and review
The way in which the proposal is working in practice should be looked at closely at the end of a term or year to make sure it is working as intended. Ideally there should be a rolling programme of review to look at all school policies and practices over several years as part of the school development process (see p 37).

If young people take part in these steps from when they start primary school, they will have little difficulty understanding the process as it applies in parliament when they study it in secondary school.

day-to-day activities as well as the curriculum and decision-making structures.

These three areas inevitably overlap, so the separation into different chapters is rather arbitrary. Chapter Four looks at what citizenship means for the school community and ethos, in terms of membership, aims and values, constitution, conflict resolution, the environment and communication. Chapter Five is about creating an empowering curriculum in the classroom, and Chapter Six outlines democratic decision-making structures. Chapter Seven summarises the step which local and national government should take to support citizenship schools.

At its most profound, citizenship education is a process through which a school transforms itself into a democratic learning community.

School citizenship parallels with the political process

The sequence of steps in this exercise has similarities with the way laws are made in Britain. A law starts as an idea. For an insider (a civil servant or minister in government) the process is much easier than for an outsider, just as it is for a head teacher or senior member of the school. Outsiders have to lobby or campaign for their idea to be adopted, as a manifesto commitment or aspiration from a political party. If the party is in power, this gets turned into a specific proposal which may be published as a Green (discussion) or a White (consultation) Paper. Laws are usually written by civil servants, following their minister's instructions. Laws are introduced in parliament in several stages - first reading, which is just the title and aims of the bill; second reading, during which it is discussed in depth; committee stage, which is like a working group; and third reading, after which it is agreed (it also has to go through both houses of parliament). The main difference from parliament is that governments seldom review their policies unless something goes wrong or there is a change of government.

This process will contribute to the following points in Citizenship Attainment Target 1 at Key Stage 4:

c) the work of parliament, the government and the courts in making and shaping the law;

d) the importance of playing an active part in democratic and electoral processes;

f) the opportunities for individuals and voluntary groups to bring about social change locally, nationally, in Europe and internationally.

Using the citizenship planning grid

The citizenship planning grid can be used in a variety of ways to develop a whole school approach to citizenship. These sheets may be easier to use if photocopied and enlarged onto A3 paper. The headings may be changed for different purposes, outlined below.

The first column sets out the national curriculum requirements, starting with the relevant elements in the PSHE primary curriculum. In practice it may be easier to start with AT 2 (Developing skills of enquiry and communication), and also with AT3 (Developing skills of participation and responsible action), then looking at AT1 (Knowledge and understanding).

Whole school planning

Use one set of sheets for the whole school to discuss and identify key features before producing separate plans for each year.

Use the second column to identify the specific needs and wants of the pupils at your school in relation to each topic. For example, AT1 b) 'the diversity of national, regional, religious and ethnic identities in the United Kingdom and the need for mutual respect and understanding' will be very different in a multi-racial school than in an all-white one.

This requires real understanding of the pupils and should be done with them. The citizenship topics can themselves be used in a card-sort exercise as described on page 7 (see page 8 for photocopiable cards).

The third column can be used to write where and how that element can be covered, such as assemblies, circle time, citizenship or PSHE classes, lessons in other subjects, community projects, visits, the schools council, the internet, or other activities.

Continued on page 41

Planning grid

This grid sets out the Attainment Targets most relevant to citizenship in the new PSHE and Citizenship Curriculum. The Primary and Secondary curriculums are in two separate grids combining Key Stages 1 and 2, and Key Stages 3 and 4 respectively. Letters a), b), c) etc are the same as in the published curriculum. Where there is a straightforward development of a point between Key Stages in either primary or secondary curriculums, the text for the next Key Stage has been added in italic within the same box. Additional points in the next Key Stage appear in separate boxes prefixed by the relevant number and letter of the published curriculum. We hope this will help schools plan across each phase and between phases.

Primary PSHE KS 1 and 2

Attainment Target 1: Developing confidence and responsibility and making the most of their abilities

Pupils should be taught:	What pupils need/want	Where/how it can be learnt	Lead person/who else involved
a) to recognise what they like and dislike, what is fair and unfair, and what is right and wrong			
b) to share *and write* about their opinions on things that matter to them and explain their views *on issues that affect them and society*			
KS2b) to recognise their worth as individuals by *identifying positive things about themselves and their achievements, seeing their mistakes, making amends and setting personal goals*			
c) to recognise, name and deal with their feelings in a positive way, *as they approach puberty, recognise, how emotions change, and how to deal positively with their feelings towards themselves, family and others*			
KS2c) to face new challenges positively by collecting *information, looking for help, making responsible choices and taking action*			
d) to think about themselves, learn from their experiences and recognise what they are good at			
e) how to set simple goals.			

Attainment Target 2: Preparing to play an active role as citizens

Pupils should be taught:	What pupils need/want	Where/how it can be learnt	Lead person/who else involved
a) to take part in discussions with one other person and the whole class			
b) to take part in a simple debate about topical issues; *research, discuss and debate topical issues, problems and events*			
c) to recognise choices they can make, and recognise the difference between right and wrong; *to realise consequences of antisocial and aggressive behaviour, such as bullying and racism, on individuals and communities*			
d) to agree and follow rules for their group and classroom, and understand how rules help them; *know why and how rules and laws are made and enforced, why they are needed in different situations, and how to take part in making and changing rules*			
e) to realise that people and other living things have needs, and that they have responsibilities to meet them			

Transforming schools through citizenship

Pupils should be taught:	What pupils need/want	Where/how it can be learnt	Lead person/who else involved
f) that they belong to various groups and communities, such as family and school; *and there are different kinds of responsibilities, rights and duties at home, at school and in the community, and that these can sometimes conflict with each other*			
g) what improves and harms their local, natural and built environments and about some of the ways people look after them			
h) to contribute to the life of the class and school			
i) to realise that money comes from different sources and can be used for different purposes; *and that resources can be allocated in different ways and that these economic choices affect individuals, communities and the sustainability of the environment*			
KS2e) *to reflect on spiritual, moral, social, and cultural issues, using imagination to understand other people's experiences*			
KS2f) *to resolve differences by looking at alternatives, making decisions and explaining choices*			
KS2g) *to know what democracy is, and about the basic institutions that support it locally and nationally*			
KS2h) *to recognise the role of voluntary, community and pressure groups*			
KS2j) *to appreciate the range of national, regional, religious and ethnic identities in the United Kingdom*			
KS2j) *to explore how the media present information.*			

Attainment Target 4: Developing good relationships and respecting the differences between people

Pupils should be taught:	What pupils need/want	Where/how it can be learnt	Lead person/who else involved
a) to recognise how their behaviour affects other people and themselves; to care about other people's feelings and try to see things from their point of view			
b) to listen to other people, and play and work cooperatively			
c) to identify and respect differences and similarities between people, *that arise from a number of factors, including cultural, ethnic, racial and religious diversity, gender and disability*			
2e) to recognise and challenge stereotypes			
2g) where individuals, families and groups can get help and support			
d) that family and friends should care for each other; *be aware of different types of relationship, including marriage and develop skills to be effective in relationships*			
e) that there are different types of teasing and bullying, that bullying is wrong, and how to get help to deal with bullying. *To realise the consequences of racism, teasing, and aggressive behaviours and how to respond to them*			

Secondary PSHE KS3 and 4
Attainment Target 1: Knowledge and understanding about becoming informed citizens

Pupils should be taught about:	What pupils need/want	Where/how it can be learnt	Lead person/who else involved
a) the legal and human rights and responsibilities underpinning society, *how they relate to citizens,* basic aspects of the criminal *and civil justice systems,* and how both relate to young people			
b) *the origins and implications of the diversity of national, regional, religious and ethnic identities in the United Kingdom and the need for mutual respect and understanding*			
c) central and local government, the public services they offer and how they are financed, and the opportunities to contribute			
d) the key characteristics of parliamentary and other forms of government; *the work of parliament, government and courts in shaping and making law*			
e) the electoral system and the importance of voting *and playing an active part in democratic processes*			
KS4e) How the economy functions, including the role of business and financial services			
f) the work of community-based, national and international voluntary groups; *opportunities for individuals and groups to bring about social change locally, nationally and internationally*			
g) the importance of resolving conflict fairly			
h) the significance of the media in society, including *the internet, in providing information and opinion; the importance of a free press*			
KS4h) rights and responsibilities of consumers, employers and employees			
i) the world as a global community, and the political, economic, environmental and social implications of this, and the role of the European Union, the Commonwealth and the UN			
KS4j) wider issues and challenges of global interdependence and responsibility, including sustainable development and Local Agenda 21,			

Attainment Target 2: Developing skills of enquiry and communication

Pupils should be taught to:	What pupils need/want	Where/how it can be learnt	Lead person/who else involved
a) think about and research topical political, spiritual, moral, social and cultural issues, problems and events by analysing information and its sources, including ICT-based sources, *showing awareness of the use and abuse of statistics*			
b) *express and justify* orally and in writing a personal opinion about such issues, problems or events			
c) contribute to group and exploratory class discussions, and take part in *formal* debates			

Attainment Target 3: Developing skills of participation and responsible action

Pupils should be taught to:	What pupils need/want	Where/how it can be learnt	Lead person/who else involved
a) use their imagination to consider other people's experiences and be able to think about, express, explain *and critically evaluate* views that are not their own			
b) negotiate, decide and take part responsibly in both school and community-based activities			
c) reflect on the process of participating.			

The fourth column can be used to identify the lead person for that activity, as well as other individuals and agencies who may be involved.

Subject planning

The grid can also be used by subject specialists to identify ways in which citizenship topics and skills can be covered across the curriculum.

In this case the second column is used to identify the relevant subject topic. A biology course for example, might look at the political debate surrounding genetically modified organisms and also consider the role of parliament and pressure groups in science. A literature course might discuss the impact of Dickens on social policy. Many topics in citizenship could be covered through history lessons and projects.

Monitoring and evaluation

The grid can also be used to help monitor and evaluate coverage of the citizenship curriculum. In this case the second column is used to note an activity (planned or impromptu), the third column to note or evaluate what happened, and the fourth to note points for future reference, or concerns about individuals. For example:

Citizenship curriculum	activity	Evaluation	Note
e) the electoral system and the importance of voting.	Election of class reps to student council. vs representative democracy.	90% participation; discussion of direct representatives to give monthly report. Student rating: 8.5	Balloting extended over second day; class asked

Students could be asked to rate activities out of ten and the results recorded as an average (see student evaluation, p 80)

Part 2: **Creating a culture of citizenship**

> **The child who is capable of forming his or her own views has the right to express those views freely in all matters affecting them.**
>
> *Article 12, The UN Convention on the Rights of the Child*

What is the school's constitution?

Most schools have a statement of aims and values, a development plan, a decision-making structure and policies covering almost everything from behaviour to the curriculum. These documents, together with its customs, norms and legal framework, make up the school's 'constitution'. Like the British constitution, it is not a single document.

An unwritten or piecemeal constitution has the advantage of flexibility; it also means that custom and powerful personalities may dominate. If the customs are sound and the personalities enlightened, the regime can be very good, as it is in many schools. If the customs are bad or the personalities ineffective, change is often impossible without a coup or revolution.

Most schools are a form of monarchy, with a great deal of power and responsibility vested in the head teacher. The governors form a privy council of advisers and the heads of department may be barons, cabinet members or vassal princes, depending on the school. Some schools are constitutional monarchies, in which the head plays a significant but ceremonial role, while others are republics, run by a powerful president appointed by the governors.

The position of pupils, parents and teachers is also defined by the school's constitution. In some schools everyone has to do what they are told, obeying a chain of command from the head down, while others have a more democratic style. In most schools, however, pupils are the subjects of education rather than active citizens in the world of learning. They are relatively powerless in the face of an established curriculum and constitution which prescribes almost every moment of their lives in school. Children who successfully conform to expectations are rewarded with praise, while those who have difficulty living up to expectations become demoralised or rebel. The way in which pupils behave is often a response to their position in the school's constitution.

A written constitution may not be essential for a citizenship school, but the process of drawing together the school's aims, values and policies in one place, where everyone can refer to them, can strengthen the purpose and cohesion of the school community. This is more powerful if all members are involved and the process culminates in a shared commitment. By giving this document authority over and above any individual, the school affirms its collective agreement. The written document becomes a benchmark against which progress can be measured. By involving everyone in reviewing and revising this document, school members learn how public participation can work, which is part of the citizenship curriculum. They also gain experience as active citizens of the school.

Writing a school constitution or student charter

A school constitution can be drawn up from existing documents, from scratch, or a mixture of both. Create a 'constitutional assembly' with representatives of all sections of the school community - pupils, parents, support staff, mainscale teachers, senior management and the community. Draw up aims for the school (using exercise on p 47), agree on different categories of membership, their rights and responsibilities, decision-making structures, from class to whole school level, and procedures for resolving disputes. Consult on these through all decision-making bodies of the school and bring it to a whole school meeting for final agreement. Create suitable ceremonies and celebrations to emphasise the significance of each stage in the process. (See discussion of the process of transformation on p 34).

A similar process can be used to draw up a 'student charter', now common in colleges and universities, and increasingly adopted by schools.

This process might include the following headings: aims, admissions, community life, academic standards, support for students, learning resources, facilities, information, freedom of speech, student voice, and redress.

Exercises like this can be linked with discussions of the Magna Carta (1215), the American Constitution, UN Charter, Universal Declaration of Human Rights, Conventional on the Rights of the Child or other constitutional events.

School citizenship

For members of a school to be citizens rather than consumers, users or subjects, they must have a real sense of their own power as learners and members of the school community. The new PSHE guidelines refer to pupils 'as members of a class and school community', while the programmes of study for citizenship include 'active involvement in the life of their school'. This implies that pupils are citizens of the school community, but the concept is not developed.

Lack of clarity about the powers and duties of different members of a school leads to very different views about democratic education. 'Free schools', like Summerhill, define citizenship as equality for pupils and teachers to make decisions at a school meeting. Other schools, like Quinton Kynaston in the mid-1980s, emphasised democracy for staff participation in decision-making. Many schools have developed student councils, often with very limited powers. In some schools pupils share decisions through circle time in each class and a school's council of representatives from every class.

Most other European countries have extensive legislation to ensure that pupils and parents are formally involved in decision-making in education, through pupil councils and parent representatives. In much of Europe, pupils and parents are represented on committees within the school, locally, regionally and nationally. In Holland, for example, parents and pupils (in secondary schools) are represented on a Participation Council, which advises the school board. Schools have both a parents' and a pupils' council. Secondary school pupils are also represented on a National Pupil Action Committee. Every school must also have a pupil charter, setting out school rules, disputes procedures, pupils' rights, and procedures for complaints, safety and maintaining the quality of teaching. Britain is unique in not having pupils on governing bodies or national structures for consultation on education policies.[17]

Our concept of citizen is relatively undeveloped, compared to that of customer or consumer. People exercise power as both customers and citizens, in the market and in politics. The role of customer varies widely, from everyday shopping to buying a house or airplane. There are markets in money, music, commodities and companies. The powers and responsibilities of participants in different markets are relatively well defined according to the scale and nature of the purchase. A citizen, on the other hand, tends to seen primarily as a voter. Unlike the customer, who is active almost every day, the 'active citizen' is an exception. However, the modern customer is also relatively new. For most of history communities looked after most of their own needs and bought much less. In future, the active citizen should become the norm, with schools playing an important part as centres of citizenship and learning.

It is therefore worthwhile working out in more detail what citizenship means for members of a school community.

The lesson most people learn from school today is powerlessness (see exercise on p 29). Everything is so highly prescribed that few people, whether pupil, parent, teacher or even the head, feel able to influence events. Changing this experience is fundamental to creating a sense of citizenship in school. Absolute civic equality, as at Summerhill, is not the only, nor necessarily the most appropriate, form of citizenship for all schools. We need more sophisticated models of citizenship appropriate to every school.

Civic equality is a fundamental principle of citizenship, but in reality there are vast differences in power and responsibility within institutions of the state, as well as within voluntary organisations and community groups. Even the vote is not equal: individual citizens in marginal constituencies have relatively more influence than those in safe seats, and politicians focus more attention on floating voters in these seats.

In legal terms, the roles and responsibility of all members of a school community are defined by acts of parliament concerning education, employment, health and safety, nationality, disability, race and gender equality, as well as UN conventions on human rights, including the Rights of the Child. The law gives head teachers a great deal of power and responsibility for running the school, while the governing body has a collective responsibility for overall direction and management.

In practice, the distribution of power and responsibility varies greatly between schools. Sometimes a staff group, the caretaker, a clique of parents or the chair of governors seem to hold sway, while in other schools power is diffused through informal consultation and tacit understanding.

As 'citizens' of a school community, pupils, parents, teachers, support staff, community users of the building and other stake holders will always have different roles and responsibilities, but these should be made explicit and consistent with democratic values.

The process of transforming members of the school community into citizens involves:

- clarifying existing powers, roles and responsibilities of different members of the school community, including pupils, parents, staff, community users of the building and other stake holders;
- ensuring that all members have the information and opportunities to exercise their powers and responsibilities; and
- providing opportunities for the school as a whole to agree how power and responsibility will be distributed, consistent with democratic values.

These steps are much the same as for creating an effective school. The main difference is that an 'effective school' tends to be seen in largely terms of good management, while a 'citizenship school' also aspires to democratic values and empowerment of the school community. Good management is necessary for citizenship to be effective, so that these models are not incompatible.

Different categories of school citizens may be identified in terms of their core rights and responsibilities:

- **Pupils** have a right (and also a responsibility) to learn, play and take part in society as young citizens. Their rights are legally set out in the Convention on the Rights of the Child, which includes the right to be heard, treated with respect and have a voice in decisions affecting them.
- **Parents** have primary responsibility for their children's education and care, and rights in relation to the school as a public service.
- **Teachers** have ultimate responsibility for securing children's right to learn, play and develop, as well as rights as employees and professionals.
- **Other staff** have various responsibilities for the emotional and physical well-being of the school community, with rights as employees and professionals distinct from those of teachers.
- **Community users** may have particular rights based on contracts with the school, as well as acts of parliament governing the community use of school premises.
- **Other stake holders,** such as the local authority, national government, tax payers, employers and local residents have various rights and responsibilities enshrined in law and custom.

All share a responsibility for learning, maintaining emotional and physical safety, participating in decisions concerning the school community and acting as a corporate citizen in the local area.

School citizenship recognises that people have quite different roles and responsibilities, but that common membership creates a shared responsibility for their own destiny as learners, teachers, carers and fellow human beings. To be effective, this shared responsibility must be underpinned by shared values.

Sustaining shared vision, values and virtues

The school's culture and ethos teaches the most powerful lesson any child will learn. Behaviour, relationships with others, attitudes to learning, values and a sense of self are strongly influenced by school life. Teaching values is an explicit part of the whole curriculum as well as citizenship, but values are not defined.

Values are what we care about. They express the 'know why' of life, knowledge and society, often at a fundamental level. While most education seems preoccupied by 'know how' and 'know what', the 'know why' is what endures when the how and what have ceased to be relevant. Values provide a reference point for thought and action. Having clear values is a powerful aid to decision-making, because they provide a quick yardstick to assess different options. A strong sense of values is also empowering for both individuals and organisations, because they know where they stand in relation to competing choices.

Values vary widely between people, cultures and organisations, leading to very different consequences for what we do. The values of wealth, status, power over others, and fame have very different implications from frugality, equality, obedience and humility. People may be motivated by fashion or a sense of justice, instant gratification or unconditional love, low prices or fair trade. In a market economy like ours, ultimate values are often reduced to self interest and economic success as measured by money, almost regardless of how it was obtained. Values such as the sacred, environmental sustainability or public service may be honoured but not acted on.

Virtues are those values which a society, school, profession or other group recognises as good. Although not a fashionable word, virtue stands for core values such as love, honesty, beauty, truth and justice. Virtues also vary according to time and custom, so that one group may value honour above all else, while another values achievement and yet another values loyalty, right or wrong. Obedience, honour, loyalty or other values may lead some people to commit what others regard as appalling crimes. Transgressions against certain virtues can be severely punished, by shame, failure or even criminal proceedings and imprisonment.

For society, a widely respected set of shared values can bring enormous benefits. They answer fundamental questions about meaning and purpose, which enables people to get on with the 'what' and 'how'. Shared values are more likely to be upheld and enforced by people themselves, reducing the need for external enforcement. Shared values also create a greater sense of social cohesion. Investing in a common core of shared values could therefore bring a greater common purpose, lower enforcement costs and greater social cohesion.

But upholding shared values is not easy at a time of rapid change, in a society with often conflicting values and people from many different traditions. The question is, what values do you impart? Although certain obvious values are clearly necessary to live within the law, those who do not share them can experience common values as oppressive. Many people have strong opinions about what values should be taught, but values change. What was once taboo becomes tolerated or even the norm, and former norms become unacceptable. In a democratic society, therefore, it is important that all members take part in affirming and shaping the values we live by.

A citizenship school, therefore, seeks to uphold a core of shared values and also to enable every individual to develop a clear sense of their own values (for a discussion of teaching values, see p 47).

Vision expresses our aims, direction or goal. While values express why we do something, a vision points to where we are going, the outcome we want to achieve. Vision and values are closely linked, but a statement of aims or vision is more specific.

Schools clearly have a central role in developing the values and visions of each generation. Religious schools obviously draw their values from a particular tradition, although even they are re-interpreted for the age. Secular schools often have a more instrumental and relativistic approach to values. Citizenship schools have a strong commitment to the democratic values of equality, mutual respect, participation and social justice.

A statement of aims, vision and values should be used actively throughout the school to reinforce agreed values and empower members of the school community in their own lives. Traditional ways of sustaining shared values, such as a motto or mission statement, songs, stories, murals, displays, assemblies, rituals and celebrations, can be made interesting and relevant to people's lives.

The best way of inspiring a spirit of shared school citizenship and morale is to give young people ownership of the class or school aims and values, through an activity like that below.

Ref 1
p 103

Peers School's vision statement

'The school aims to promote the full potential of learning for every student, in the expectation that this will be both great and varied, in all school activities and in a variety of contexts. The primary means for achieving this is through the structure, content and organisation of the school curriculum.

'It is the aim of the school that the students be empowered to take decisions about their lives in a democracy. The decisions they take while at school, about their own learning for example, are part of this process.

'The learning process in Peers is seen as a part of lifelong education. The careers programme is planned in a way that acknowledges this, and the school facilities are open to people of all ages.

'It is the aim of the school to recognise and value achievement across the range of human capabilities, the academic, practical, creative and physical.'

Developing shared aims and values

Many schools have a statement of aims and values. The aim of this exercise is to give members of the school an opportunity to reflect on the values they experience in school and to express the values to which they aspire. A similar format can be used to develop shared aims.

The exercise can be used to introduce new pupils, parents and staff to the school's values at the start of the academic year, to review aims and values as part of the school development and planning process, or to create a statement of values for each class. Obviously this exercise needs to be adapted to the circumstances in which it is used and the age of participants.

Take a few minutes to discuss the nature of values, giving a few examples such as truth, honesty, respect, loyalty, courage, trust, justice, equality and environmental sustainability. (See list on p 46). If appropriate, present the current statement of aims and values, or the new national curriculum statement.

Ask each person to write down the values they experience at school. With young children, ask them to say how they feel they are treated by others in school (or what they see as the aims of the school – 'what's the point of coming to school?').

Then ask people to form groups of four or five to compare lists and draw up a joint list of the values, in the order of importance as they experience them. Then ask all groups to share their lists, to see what consensus exists across the school. Different groups are likely to have very different experiences, which usually creates conflict or tension that may be hidden.

If this is the case, it is very important to spend some time bringing the values of different sections of the school community into alignment, by ensuring that everyone knows and understands what its values are or by changing the values, or by a bit of both.

To find out what values people want, ask each person to write down a list of values that they want the school to live by.

A useful refinement at this point is to ask each group (or individual) to chose one to three values that are particularly important to them, and to give a brief presentation on them to the whole group, saying what they mean and why they are important, giving examples from life.

Then ask people to form groups of four or five to compare lists and draw up a joint list of the values, in the order of importance. This can be done by writing values on cards and putting them in order. Then get the whole group to draw up a joint list.

If the group is large, prioritisation can be done by 'dot voting': give each person three, five or seven coloured stickers to put onto the joint list of values, each one representing a vote. Ask them to put the stickers against those values they see as most important (people can put more than one sticker on values they rate highly).

Finally, ask the whole group to create a short sentence or paragraph to express the top three to seven values.

For a whole-school process, it may be necessary to use this result to guide any working group or consultation process on school values.

The core values identified should be posted where they can be clearly seen and referred to at any time. During the school year, children can be encouraged to express these values in poetry, pictures, songs or plays, as well as apply them in their daily lives.

A similar process can be used to develop a statement of class or school aims and vision.

Transitions

The arrival and departure of each generation of school students should be momentous events in the life of any school. Young people are its reason for being. They bring fresh eyes, new hopes and expectations. When they leave, they take insights and experience from school into the world, like the seeds of a dandelion (see Moving on, p 60).

Welcoming each new intake needs a lot of care and attention. Whenever we go somewhere new, our instinctive response is likely to be anxiety or fear. The brain becomes alert to danger and screens out all information not relevant for survival. This prevents children (and adults) from learning. Preparation and induction

for new pupils and their parents is therefore a vital foundation for learning citizenship. It is the moment when their membership of the school community is defined and sets a pattern for the future. For each child, it can set a pattern for their entire lives.

Starting and leaving school are defining moments in people's lives. Each year is the first and last year for a substantial proportion of the school community. As the world becomes increasingly mobile, with people moving jobs, homes and schools more often than ever, it is particularly important for schools to make these transitions a significant experience. Every transition is an opportunity for people to reflect on their past experiences and prepare for a new stage in their lives.

For citizenship schools, the start of each school year is an opportunity to welcome new members into a democratic learning community, and to share ownership of its values, purpose and ethos. The end of the year is an opportunity to evaluate the whole of the experience for each person leaving and to celebrate their individual contributions to the school. In future the start and finish of the school year could become blurred, as mobility increases and timetables become more flexible. This makes the moments of transition for each individual even more important.

One way of valuing the fresh eyes of a new group of pupils, or new staff, is to invite them to act as consultants. As part of their induction, a new group of pupils or a staff member could be asked to do a survey of the school. This could be a general review, inviting them to list everything they like or which seems to work well and to identify things that do not work, or it could be a specific review, looking at an aspect of the school such as playtimes, recycling, the movement of people in a particular area, the use of a staff room or particular classroom. In either case, the aim is to observe, listen, describe, draw conclusions and make recommendations. This has the advantage of giving the newcomer in-depth insights and ownership of change early in their school career, while giving the school free consultancy and an opportunity for improvement. However, it is important that newcomers are able to present their findings to a safe and sympathetic listener, such as a mentor or a peer, so that they can be both honest about what they see and not be embarrassed if they misinterpret what they see. Both outcomes can be valuable to the school. (See also Students as Researchers, p 72

Most of this section is about welcoming new pupils and parents, but many of these issues also apply to new staff, for whom the process of appointment, induction and acceptance by the school community is equally important. It requires equal care and consideration, whatever their position.

Welcome to a citizenship school

First impressions are lasting impressions. Successful transition from pre-school to primary, and primary to secondary, the school needs to create in each pupil and parent a sense of

Induction week at Highfield Junior

Highfield Junior uses induction weeks to establish boundaries and expectations of behaviour, to create understanding and empathy within the class (including the teacher), and to lessen the need for control other than that imposed by oneself and the group. All decisions are negotiated with the children through circle time and a democratic approach, once the outline school parameters have been clearly established. Induction takes up to two weeks in term one, up to one week for recap and renegotiation in term two, and two days recap in term three. "This may seem a huge allocation of time" say the school guidelines, but we "believe that setting this firm foundation of ownership, pride and self-responsibility strengthens the children's will, capacity and tenacity to learn, to produce acceptable patterns of behaviour and to share practical group activities which lead to positive outcomes."[18]

Induction weeks give children time to settle in, establish their work, what they want and class aims. "They listen to my needs as a teacher. I listen to their needs, and we sort things out. Circle times have been brilliant for that." They involve children in finding out what needs to be done in school, writing job descriptions, allocating jobs and then carrying them out, with elected House Captains taking responsibility for rules and behaviour in school.[19]

- acceptance (I am welcome and worthwhile);
- capability (my abilities are valued);
- safety and security (I will come to no harm);
- anticipation (I have a purpose here, I am going to enjoy it);
- participation (I can speak up and do things I want to do);
- responsibility (I have a part to play, which is important and depends on me);
- belonging (this is my place);
- integrity (I don't need to pretend to be something I am not).

Each of these points can be used to plan activities for pupils' induction, such as the following:

- safe routes to school – Information on getting to school, or even personal guidance by an older pupil;
- treasure hunt and orientation exercises in the school buildings and playgrounds;

A citizen's welcome

Pupils should be taught to realise that people and other living things have needs, and that they have responsibilities to meet them

PSHE Key Stage 1, AT 2e (Preparing to play an active role as citizens)
(See also KS 2, AT 2d) and Citizenship, AT 3b) for KS 3 and 4)

This activity aims to involve pupils in welcoming the new intake to the school. It may be used for primary, middle or secondary pupils. It could be used as part of a peer support or buddy system for new pupils. It can take 40 to 90 minutes, and can be done shortly after pupils have arrived or when preparing for the new intake.

The opening steps can be done in circle time. Older pupils could lead the activity in secondary school, with a class council or student council.

Start by asking pupils to remember how they felt when they first came to school. You could do a short guided visualisation. Ask them to close their eyes and speak slowly, saying something along the following lines:

"Relax your mind. Can you remember when you first heard that you were coming to this school? PAUSE What were your first thoughts and feelings about coming to this school? PAUSE Where did you get your first impressions from? Was it from your parents? Pupils at the school? From the school itself? PAUSE Can you remember when you first visited this school? What did you do? Who did you see? PAUSE Did you choose to come to this school? Or did your parents decide for you? What helped you or them decide to come here? PAUSE Remember how you felt on your first day at school. PAUSE What did you do? PAUSE Who did you talk with? PAUSE What helped you most when you started school? PAUSE Take a moment to relive your first week at school. PAUSE And when you are ready, slowly open your eyes and bring yourself back into the present."

Ask them to turn to the person next to them, decide which one is A and B, then ask B to tell A about their experience of starting school, while A listens. After 3-5 minutes, check that Bs have had enough time and ask them to change over.

As a class, go through the questions in the guided visualisation, asking pupils how they felt and noting key words on the board. Make sure everyone contributes and you get a representative picture by asking after each contribution 'how many other children felt like that?'

Once everyone has a shared sense of how it felt like to start school, ask them to discuss ways of improving the process in pairs. Ask each pair to come up with at least one idea of how to make starting school more interesting and welcoming. Take suggestions from the group, writing them on the board and with each suggestion ask how many others had similar ideas.

Thank them for their suggestions and ask if they would like to help organise the welcome for new pupils.

As an extension to this exercise, use the list of bulleted suggestions (page 49) under the heading 'Welcome to a Citizenship School'. Ask pupils to suggest ways new attendees to the school can be made welcome. This can lead to a variety of activities such as pupils drawing and writing cards to each new person arriving; pupils organising an exhibition of life at school for prospective pupils and parents; a treasure hunt and orientation exercises in the school and grounds; and setting up a 'buddy' or befriending scheme.

- doing up a form room;
- reviewing work done in preparatory activities (or catching up if not done);
- providing intensive coaching for critical weaknesses in literacy or numeracy;
- displaying achievements and prized objects from home or primary schools;
- playing icebreakers and trust games with staff;

- drawing up classroom rules and sanctions;
- setting up a 'buddy' or befriending scheme;
- introducing older students as mentors or advisers for individuals or small groups;
- developing individual responsibilities.

Parents also need to be actively welcomed into the school community as early as possible through initiation activities that enable them to overcome barriers and form close relationships with other parents and staff, such as:

■ a welcome evening and social for all new parents and students early in the first year to meet each other, staff and some active parents from other years;
■ a 'class meeting' to introduce parents in each class and create mutual support round issues such as transport to school, after-school clubs, excursions and other

activities (see below);
■ drawing up a home-school agreement (see following exercise).

The importance of the personal attention given to new members, as learning citizens, into the school community cannot be over-emphasised. This experience creates expectations and relationships for the rest of their school career. An indifferent start can take a lot of effort to overcome later. A positive and personal welcome creates great expectations.

A citizenship approach to home-school agreements

This exercise can be used to involve parents in drawing up a home-school agreement as a class or year. It can be used as a topic for a class meeting (see p 92) before children start school or early in their first term. It aims to create mutual understanding and trust through a class-centred whole school approach to working with parents as educational partners. It takes 45-90 minutes.

The process of producing a home-school agreement is widely recognised as being more valuable than the written document or the act of signing. This exercise therefore involves parents and teachers of each class in drawing up an agreement.

It can be done with all parents of a whole class, sitting in groups of four to six, together with the teachers, governors and other members of the school community who will work with that class. For secondary schools it can involve pupils as well.

Each group takes on the role of either children, parents or school (taken to mean staff and governors). As far as possible, people should join the group appropriate to their role in the school. Each group should address one of the following sets of questions, for about 20 minutes:

Exploring expectations

Children:
1. What do children want and need from the school?

2. What do children offer the school?

3. What does the school offer children?

Parents:
1. What do parents want from the school?

2. What do parents offer the school?

3. What does the school offer parents?

School:
1. What does the school want from parents?

2. What does the school offer parents?

3. What does the school want from children?

4. What does the school offer children?

Each group then presents their responses to the questions to the whole group. Other groups can ask questions, but there is no discussion until all groups have been heard. Whole group discussion is optional. Each group then spends about ten minutes revising their response in the light of what other groups have said. Each group then chooses one or two people to form a single group to draft a home-school agreement. This group should include at least one parent, one teacher, one governor and, in secondary schools, two pupils.

Agreements drawn up in this way will be different every year, but pupils, parents, teachers and issues facing the community are different every year. In one year the main concern might be reading skills or behaviour, while another year might be troubled by drugs or violence.

This agreement can be revisited by each class once a year or between each key stage.

See also Partnerships with parents, p 65

Creating community and responsibility

Pupils take part in school and community-based activities, demonstrating personal and group responsibility in their attitudes to themselves and others.
Citizenship Curriculum, End of Key Stage Descriptor (and AT 3b)

Safety is the first concern of any community. Emotional and physical safety are preconditions for productive learning. People will learn when under stress or in danger, but what they learn is often conditioned by stress and danger, which can cause depression when danger is absent.

Some essential requirements for a healthy, happy school community are:
■ clear expectations and fair rules or boundaries for behaviour;
■ positive benefits for upholding agreed boundaries;
■ consistent sanctions when they are breached;
■ effective ways of resolving conflicts (such as peer mediation);
■ effective ways of expressing and meeting needs (such as circle time and student councils);
■ recognition for achievement and contributions to the community;
■ celebration of personal and shared milestones, such as birthdays, religious festivals, anniversaries and other occasions.

In a citizenship school, everyone is involved in community building as a democratic process. Each member of the community develops discipline from within. Teachers intervene to help pupils learn self-discipline. Where physical safety is threatened or the situation is out of control, firm and decisive intervention is necessary, but the aim is to use every opportunity to develop self-discipline so that the school community is self-managing and situations do not go out of control.

Fair rules

School rules are often our first experience of a system of justice. This experience colours our whole understanding and relationship with the law. If the rules are arbitrary, excessively harsh or imposed from outside, children will see the law in these terms. For them, law is not the collective discipline of a self-governing society, which can be changed by citizens acting together, but an alien force. As a result, some young people see law breaking as an act of self-determination and punishment as just bad luck.

At the other extreme, if children experience disorder, unresolved conflict and an absence of rules, they may get away with anything for a time, but will be utterly unprepared for the discipline of a world in which punishment means fines or imprisonment.

In the absence of external rules, children develop their own systems of justice. Children are a majority in the weekly meetings that govern Summerhill School, which usually has over 100 rules. Since most children grow up in a rule-governed world, they tend to recreate rules, punishments and rewards they know from their family, school and community.

Equality under the law and human rights are fundamental principles of citizenship. The citizenship curriculum includes 'the legal and human rights and responsibilities underpinning society, including basic aspects of the criminal justice system'.

Citizenship schools therefore ensure that children and all members of the school community:
■ take part in making the rules that apply to them;
■ share in upholding and enforcing school rules;
■ are treated equally, unless the rules make clear exceptions, such as a smoking room for adults, or no queuing at dinner for staff or students on playground duty.

Children are very quick to spot unfairness or partiality, and will often accept punishment with good grace if they feel it is deserved. They are also more likely to respect rules which they themselves have agreed. But often children see school rules as unfair and unjustly applied. In particular, they often observe different rules being applied to adults and themselves, or between teachers and support staff or parents.

Behaviour is a learned skill like any other. Often children are inadvertently taught disruptive or inappropriate behaviour by adults, because the only way in which a child can get their needs met is to cause a disturbance.

Rules, boundaries and supported self-discipline

Rules are a way of maintaining safe boundaries to protect all members of the school community. Boundaries describe limits. They may be negotiable, such as the length of time to complete a project or homework, or absolute, like the starting time of lessons and other events. The important thing is that they are clear and consistent. Establishing boundaries helps to create emotional safety, for staff as well as students. They show people that the school community is serious about its values and principles.

Self-discipline means that each person in the school community knows what the boundaries are and agrees to stay within them. Supported self-discipline means creating rewards and privileges, which are lost when the boundaries are crossed. Threats are replaced by promises: instead of repeating the negative consequences of non-compliance, school members emphasise the positive results of staying within the agreed boundary.

Ref 2
p 104

Conflict resolution

Preventing conflicts is the work of politicians; establishing peace is the work of education.
Maria Montessori

Teachers are peacemakers. From the start of the school day they deflect, mediate or suppress conflict between pupils. Teachers have a powerful influence on the atmosphere in school and classroom. If the ethos of the school is competitive, stressful, intolerant, rigid, fearful or authoritarian, there is likely to be more conflict than if the ethos is co-operative, calm, accepting, flexible, trusting and respectful. But even in the most peaceful school, there will be conflict, between pupils and among other members of the community.

Conflict is a necessary and often valuable dimension of citizenship. Mahatma Gandhi once described conflict as a bond between the people involved. The challenge is to

Creating discipline is like making a garden

Highfield Junior describes how their first step was to 'gain control and create boundaries within which we could teach and the children could learn.'[20] The discipline in the school is like making a garden ready for the seeds of change, instead of trying to sow them in a desert or jungle. The rules become the walls of the garden. Once calm was established, the children said "We like this. But we'll always cause problems because we don't like adults ordering us to do things." So the teachers decided to make the school a democracy, involving pupils in decisions through circle time.

Circle time has four rules, which are written on the wall and repeated by children at the start of each session to remind themselves:
- Only talk one at a time
- Be kind and don't say anything that will hurt somebody
- Listen carefully
- Talk clearly so everyone can hear you.

Circle time is used for many things (see p 83), but agreeing class rules is one of the first activities. "Every year now, the children mainly choose the same rules because we know they work. Each class can add other rules if they wish."

There is one main rule for the whole school: "Show care and respect for yourself, your friends, your teachers and helpers, your belongings, your school and your family at all times."

Each class has about six rules and five for the playground, including 'No teasing, spitting, bulldog or stingray'. The teachers tried to encourage children to use positive words, but they insisted that it wouldn't have the same effect.

"Instead of me having to try to force them to keep the rules, now on the whole they wanted to keep them, and to help each other to keep to them. After all, they were their rules, not mine!" Class teacher

As children get older, they distinguish between rules and convention, which is described as a rule that 'is sort of inside you, and you would keep it anyway. One class decided, after quite a long debate, to make all rules conventions, except one 'Follow all adult instructions'.

transform conflict from a struggle between enemies, in which one side must win, into a problem, where both sides seek a solution in which there are no losers. The parties to any conflict choose whether to fight or to solve a problem. At Highfield Junior, for example, children are taught to see their behaviour as a choice, between fighting and working out a solution. They learn how to take responsibility for their behaviour by developing alternative, more constructive strategies.

In most schools, teachers contain, suppress or manage conflict from a position of authority, and most do so fairly and effectively. Order is essential for teaching to take place. In citizenship schools, reducing conflict is part of the learning process for pupils and parents as well as staff. Although the goal is the same - a calm, peaceful environment for learning - the means are different. In many schools conflict is displaced, into the playground, street or society. It can be suppressed for a while, but it is likely to erupt elsewhere. In citizenship schools people learn how to express themselves so that conflict is constructive, the underlying issues are addressed and they develop the ability to handle differences without conflict.

Teachers' justified concern about abuse, lack of respect or even violence from pupils (and sometimes parents) has to be dealt with by school communities through education, because dealing with conflict is part of the curriculum. Schools have to take a lead in learning how to resolve conflict and violence among young people, because they are best placed to work with them. Teachers cannot do it alone, just as they cannot teach effectively without parental support. But excluding children displaces the problem, or even creates a greater problem for society as children on the streets learn the ways of crime.

Training in non-violent communication, assertiveness and mediation are three ways in which schools can help people express differences effectively and handle conflict creatively. Trainers such as the Learning Foundation use puppets to illustrate violent (Jackal) and non-violent (Giraffe) ways of saying things. These imaginative approaches to learning were developed for training in industry and are as affective with adults as children. They reduce bullying, increase self-esteem and improve communication through compassion.

Non-violent communication

In any situation of actual or potential conflict, non-violent communication aims to focus on four aspects of what is going on:
1. **observation:** notice what is actually happening, and if possible describe it without judgement;
2. **feelings:** listen to what the other is feeling, or state what you are feeling, without blame;
3. **needs:** hear what the other needs, or state your needs, without making a demand or guilt trip;
4. **request:** ask what the other wants, or make a specific request, in order to make life better.

This seemingly simple four-point model can be challenging to learn and demanding to apply, but it can be learned by children as well as adults to give them a way of listening and speaking that inspires empathy and helps to prevent violence. See *Nonviolent Communication* by Marshall B Rosenberg.[21]

Learning and teaching about conflict resolution is almost impossible from a book, talk or even discussion. It needs to use games, circle time, lessons and creative intervention every time a conflict breaks out (those 'teachable moments' when a real life situation offers opportunities for deeper learning). There are many games and exercises to develop the skills of conflict resolution and a culture of co-operation.

Ref 3
p 104

The following activities offer ways of involving young people in sharing responsibility for resolving conflict and promoting peace at school:

Prefects, playground patrols or **guardian angels** are ways of involving pupils in rapid interventions to break-up fights and keep the peace. **Prefects** are usually older pupils who take turns in being 'on duty' in the playground. In citizenship schools they are either elected or all pupils in a particular year take turns on prefect duty. **Guardian angels** are a way of supporting an individual pupil who is experiencing difficulties and wants to change. They can be set up in circle time or by the teacher (or head teacher) with the pupils directly involved. A child having difficulties, because they are being bullied, are bullying others, or cannot control their temper, chooses up to three 'guardian angels' to help them. The guardian angel will fly to the rescue when a situation flares up

Creating a culture of citizenship

and help to mediate on the spot, or bring those involved to a point where they can seek mediation. In many schools house points are given where the behaviour of an individual improves, so everyone benefits.

Mediation is a valuable tool for all members of the school community. Mediation requires both partners to be willing to take part. It works when emotions have cooled and both partners are willing to negotiate. This makes it essential to actively promote the potential of mediation as a means of resolving conflict and to train enough people in mediation. Children in particular can help to resolve conflicts on a spectacular scale, if the training and support are provided on a systematic basis.

The value of mediation is that it can address feelings underlying conflicts. It has been described as a means of dealing with the iceberg of emotions and issues below the surface, in contrast to behaviour management that often only deals with issues appearing above the surface. Mediation is a powerful tool for reducing exclusions.

Peer mediation is a well developed method of training pupils from the age of seven upwards to resolve conflicts themselves. The benefits of peer mediation are that it gives pupils a powerful life time ability to resolve conflicts. This ability helps to reduce depression as well as violence.

There are a variety of models of mediation, involving one or two mediators. They broadly follow the steps set out in the exercise below or the illustration from Highfield Junior.

Mediation in practice

At Highfield Junior, a number of pupils in each class are trained in mediation and two of them are on duty in the playground every day. The process involves the mediator asking both children involved in a dispute to listen to each other talk through a sequence of steps:

- My problem is... /I want ... /I need ...
- I feel ..
- The reason is ...
- I think you want or feel ..
- Maybe we could try ...
- Let's choose ...

Understanding and resolving conflict

This three-part exercise can be used with students, staff or parents to introduce the ideas and process of mediation, either as one session or as separate exercises.

1. Conflict causes and consequences
- Ask participants to discuss in pairs actions that cause conflicts in the school.
- Ask the group to share, list the all actions and then ask each person to identify the three that concern them most.
- Ask pairs or small groups to take one of the top concerns and identify a) possible causes of the action and the conflict, b) possible consequences if the conflict is not resolved.
- List causes: conflicts can be over resources, needs (including achievement, affection, affiliation, attention, power) and beliefs (including values, rules and perception). The core causes can stem from situations of inequality, competition, hurt or humiliation (past or present) or fear.
- Discuss experiences of conflict and ask people how they tend to respond to conflict.
- Identify common responses to conflict: fight, flight, get help (alliances), capitulate, ignore it, joke about it, talk it out, seek to understand the other view point - discuss the advantages and disadvantages of each one.

2. Conflict escalators and de-escalators
- Take a relevant example of a conflict (prepared or from the discussion), draw an escalator or stairs, and ask people to say what kind of remarks will escalate it, and write the points against each step. Then ask people to identify the kind of things which escalate conflict, eg:
  - increased emotion (anger, frustration);
  - increased threat (verbal or physical);
  - people get increasingly personal about each other;
  - more people get involved on one side or other;

• other issues get drawn in (which may be irrelevant to the original issue).

● Ask people to suggest different remarks which would have reduced conflict, then discuss what will de-escalate conflict, eg
  • decrease in emotional energy ('cooling off');
  • reduced threat;
  • presence of a neutral or more powerful force;
  • focus attention on the problem, not the participants;
  • shared commitment to finding a solution (ie recognising the cost of win-lose strategies);
  • re-framing or redefining the problem to seek a win-win solution.

Conclude with a discussion of the lessons for how to deal with conflict in school.

3. Mediation process

Talk through the mediation process. Mediation requires a neutral mediator to help the people involved resolve the conflict themselves. The mediator does not to say who is right or wrong. Peer mediation often involves two children as mediators, one of whom takes the lead with the other providing support and feedback. In difficult disputes, mediators can hold private sessions with each party separately at any point to explore issues in depth and enable them to share information or change position without loss of face.

The process follows fairly well-defined steps:

1. Set the scene: the mediator outlines the process, confirms that both sides are willing to take part and agree to the ground rules. These are that each person takes turns to speak and listen, talk about yourself and do not insult the other. The mediator outlines their role, which means not taking sides, not judging, helping the participants to decide what to do without giving advice, and keeping confidentiality.

2. Hear the story: each side presents the situation as they see it without interruption or blaming. The mediator listens and summarises each person's position.

3. Define the problem: the mediator asks questions to clarify issues and understand each person's needs, wants and interests (what really matters to them). Each side can also respond to the other and ask questions to explore feelings, perceptions and information.

4. Set the agenda and acknowledge feelings: the mediator summarises the problem and issues that need to be discussed, and asks if each party can understand the other and acknowledge their feelings.

5. Explore solutions and common ground: the mediator asks each participant to suggest common ground and possible ways of solving the problem so that both gain, and both explore advantages and disadvantages of each point.

6. Build agreement: find the solution people most like, then write it down.

7. Explore consequences: discuss what could and should happen if the agreement breaks down, and what can be done to ensure that it does not.

8. Review the agreement: go through the written agreement, check that the partners understand it, see it as realistic and are committed to it. All parties sign it.

9. Follow-up: the mediators, or adult co-ordinators, check with each party to make sure the agreement is working. This can be between a day and a month after the session. Serious conflicts may need to be followed up over a longer period.

Problem solved. Mediators are not judges and the solutions come from, and are agreed by, the participants in the conflict.

Participants can practice mediation, using simulated conflicts, with one person mediating, two partners in conflict, and one person observing to give feedback at the end.

The three Rs of restorative justice

The system of justice in a citizenship school aims to help young people learn how to restore justice. The aim is the same – to maintain justice and peace by developing self-discipline and a deeper understanding of the consequences of doing wrong. Unlike 'no blame' approaches, restorative justice does not mean that wrongdoers evade responsibility.

When a pupil complains of an injustice, breaks a rule or is involved in a fight, the first step is to listen. As in non-violent communication or mediation, you first need to hear the story and understand why it happened from the point of view of those involved. There is always a need, a reason, behind behaviour. If that is not addressed, the behaviour is likely to be repeated, however severe the punishment.

While the underlying need has to be addressed, it does not justify wrongdoing. If a rule has been broken or someone has been hurt, it is important that consequences follow. The wrongdoer has to take responsibility for their actions and then make reparations for what they have done. Understanding and forgiveness are not enough. Justice requires that there must be amends.

Thus the process of restorative justice involves:

1. Recognition of the **reasons** behind the action, the needs driving the behaviour, which may need to be addressed separately.
2. The perpetrator takes **responsibility** for their actions and accepts that they have done wrong.
3. The perpetrator makes **reparations**, which means making amends for what has been done, including restitution, restoration and reconciliation to settle differences.

In restorative justice, the aim is to find out what happened, find out who and what was hurt or damaged (including the perpetrator), and what is needed to heal the situation. The aim is to establish justice in a way that everyone involved learns and grows, amends are made, and peace is restored. The strength of this approach is that people learn how to take responsibility for their actions, they learn how not to repeat their mistakes, and peace becomes stronger.

This approach can challenge more traditional, retributive forms of discipline, in which the aim is to identify the crime, find out who did it, and punish the perpetrator. The weaknesses of this approach are that both victim and victimiser are hurt, the victim does not get any compensation, the perpetrator does not deal with the underlying reasons and often does not learn how to avoid repeating the offence. As a result, retributive justice tends to increase fear and insecurity all round. The fact that crime continues to rise after centuries of retributive justice, and that most people leaving prison re-offend, suggests that alternative approaches deserve attention.

Ref 3
p 104

Maintaining the physical environment

For many pupils, school is a place they pass through. They may feel at home in primary school, but they are temporary tenants in buildings that belong to teachers or the local authority. In secondary school they are often nomads, moving from room to room with nowhere to call their own. Yet the school buildings and grounds only exist for them.

Pupils are capable of looking after and improving their environment, while learning a huge variety of practical and academic subjects.

Looking after the physical environment also creates a sense of ownership and provides opportunities for pupils to make a visible difference, so that when they leave each one can point to something and say 'I did that'. In particular, it gives everyone an opportunity to do something well, not just the most academically able.

Ref 4
p 105

Eco-committee in action

Pupils at St Paulinus Primary in Crayford, Kent review the environmental impact of the school every year. A plan is then drawn up by the 'eco-committee' of children, governors and parents. Parents and children created a nature area, which is looked after by groups of children. A reception class planted a hazel walk and bower, year six water flowers in the bird garden, a butterfly garden is tended by another group. Inside the school children do projects on waste recycling, energy use and environmental purchasing.

Planning for pupil responsibility

Identifying and sustaining pupil responsibilities for the environment requires planning and organisation, in which pupils can play a leading part. The secrets of making it happen are:

- involve pupils from the moment they start at school, if not before;
- make it a requirement for every pupil, a condition of membership;
- enable pupils to choose their own tasks as far as possible;
- link responsibilities to the curriculum where applicable;
- ensure that responsibilities are well-defined and understood by those who take them on;
- provide supervision and support, if possible involving older pupils, with adult back-up;
- review and reallocate responsibilities regularly, preferably once a term;
- acknowledge every contribution and systematically reward all good work. Ideally, pupils themselves should also identify and acknowledge good work.

Different spaces offer pupils different kinds of responsibility. The following exercise suggests how pupils might explore their feelings about the school site and take responsibility for specific spaces.

Improving playtimes

Playgrounds and playtimes can fill a fifth or more of a child's life at school. It is here that relationships are formed and broken, most bullying takes place, and children are in charge of their own time. Playtime can be the dominant experience of a child's life at school. What happens here is far more likely to be discussed with peers or parents than any lesson. Playground activities also affect learning in the classroom, and changes in the activities, organisation or layout of playgrounds can have a significant impact on behaviour and attainment in school. Pupils can play a major part in improving playtimes and playgrounds, to create 'landscapes for learning'.

Ref 5
p 106

Developing responsibilities

Most schools give some students specific responsibilities within the school community. The aim of this exercise is to ensure that every student has a specific and meaningful responsibility for which they are accountable.

Before doing this exercise, it is essential to ensure that all staff support it and are willing to help pupils take responsibility. It is particularly important that support staff see this as a way of assisting their work, not of replacing them with cheap labour. This means following the process for developing policy and practice on page 36.

In primary schools staff will need to be more directive at the start, but children can take increasing responsibility for choosing tasks in years 4, 5 or 6. In secondary schools it is best introduced in year 7, although pupils in later years can help to set it up.

There are several stages to the exercise:
● Identify every specific job (responsibility) that a pupil could do, give it a name or title, describe the purpose of the job, a short description of what is involved and the standard expected.
● Develop a process for allocating responsibilities (by choice, lot, interview or other methods) for each new intake of pupils and for pupils who join during the year.
● Develop an induction, training and support process, which could involve peer training and mentoring by older pupils.
● Develop a system of monitoring and accountability, including rewards or privileges for work well done and penalties work not done.
● Set up a disputes and appeals mechanism if necessary.

These are developed in more detail below.

As far as possible, the entire process should be run by pupils, through the student council and circle or form time. Teachers, governors, parents or other staff should play a guiding, supportive role, giving pupils lots of positive feedback and celebrating success through assemblies and special events. Adults should also provide quality assurance for the whole system, by monitoring the self-assessment or quality assurance by pupils.

Identifying areas of responsibility
The first task is to identify and describe every possible task in the school that can be done by pupils. There are different types of tasks, such as:
● Rotas, such as reception, prefects, playground or dinner duties, stewarding for parents' evenings, etc.
● Areas, such as looking after:
  • classroom display, storage or organisation;
  • display in public spaces, corridors and reception;
  • libraries and learning resources areas;
  • administration;
  • toilets and other utility areas;
  • grounds and nature areas.
● Community services, such as peer mediation, schools council, recycling, newsletters, running a community lunch, etc.
● Special tasks, such as looking at energy use by the school, student investigations, or internships with a department or specialist area, such as the library or resource room.

Allocating or choosing responsibilities
Tasks can be allocated in a variety of ways, which can also be fun:
● by lot, picking names (or tasks) out of a hat;
● task auction: tasks are described and pupils bid for them;
● pupils sign up on a list of tasks;
● through form meetings.

When the system is first set up, the pupils involved in identifying tasks can decide amongst themselves what they want to do. In subsequent years, pupils can present the task to new pupils and act as mentors or advisors.

It is easiest if groups of tasks are allocated to a particular class, who share collective responsibility for ensuring that all tasks are done well. Some sets of tasks can be allocated to particular years, for example, reception rotas are run by year 6 in primary or year 8 in secondary.

Monitoring, review and recognition

It is important for tasks to be monitored, by staff or by older pupils, and for pupils to receive recognition, through school assemblies, newsletters and in person, with special forms of recognition for achievement or effort. Recognition can also be given through 'internal currencies', like LETS (local economic trading schemes).

Sustaining commitment

Setting up a whole-school system of responsibilities takes time and commitment. In the first years it needs active encouragement and constant attention to detail. All sorts of problems will crop up and solutions found. Once the system is set up, it needs a fresh burst of energy every year and each child needs to experience a real sense of recognition and achievement for what they do, or it will become a chore.

Although sharing responsibilities among all pupils can help staff with many routine tasks and will bring about sustained improvements in the school, the system requires constant care and maintenance. A senior member of staff has to have overall responsibility, with the time to monitor how things are going, to help solve problems and to keep up enthusiasm.

The Pledge Tree

Tim Brighouse, Chief Education Officer for Birmingham, describes a lovely activity created by primary schools in Cole Heath, Birmingham, called the Pledge Tree. The 'tree' is a structure to which children of year 5 and 6 attached pledges to maintain, cherish and develop the environment, in the school and the community. Each pledge is related to a specific building, open space, pillar box or mosque. The children take care of their pledged corner of the world, talk about it, learn about its past and imagine its future.

Communications

Developing skills of enquiry and communication; Pupils should be taught to:
a) think about topical political, spiritual, moral, social and cultural issues, problems and events by analysing information and its sources, including ICT-based sources;
b) justify orally and in writing a personal opinion about such issues, problems or events;
c) contribute to group and exploratory class discussions, and take part in debates.
Citizenship Curriculum, Attainment Target 2, Key Stage 3

In citizenship schools, listening, discussing, writing and other communication skills are recognised as important activities which have an impact on people's lives. Pupils listen and talk about their own feelings in circle time (p 83), student councils (p 84) and assembly. They share their experiences and learning through story telling, newsletters, presentations and drama. They use communication skills when taking part in discussions of the school development plan and other policies, when doing community projects or taking part in model United Nations.

The most important thing about communication is that people are heard and the message has some power to move, engage or inspire the listener. Young people often feel that they will only be heard if they are extreme. It is therefore important to take young people's views seriously and engage with them constructively.

Young people need to be actively involved in meaningful communications at all times:
■ in classroom discussions about the values, meaning and purpose of subjects;
■ in discussion groups or debating societies, held in lunch breaks or after school;
■ through newsletters or magazines for the class, year, school, a specific subject or the local community.

Every meeting is a transformation.
Objibway (Native American) saying

A school newsletter can be produced by an editorial team of pupils, with adult support. Some schools produce a community newsletter for their catchment area, distributed to every door by pupils, funded through advertising, and providing a lively commentary on life at school and the local area. In some schools pupils produce specialist magazines on the arts, nature, music or sport. The important thing is that pupils have the autonomy, responsibility and resources to have a go. Beyond school, children from 8 to 18 can take part in *Children's Express*.

■ School radio, video or cable television gives pupils first hand experience of working in these powerful media.
■ Youth Cable Television involves young people from 11 to 19 in training and producing a half hour daily television programme for Nickleodeon, as well as drama and film for the BBC and other stations. TYCV runs training programmes for schools as well as members.
■ The worldwide web and email offer a whole new world of communication, with many pupils and schools setting up websites. A few pupils have even made fortunes from their own internet companies.
■ Drama can be as powerful for exploring issues today as it was in ancient Greece. Theatre in Education addresses many of the issues raised in this book and can be used across the curriculum. Plays like Brecht's *Galileo* explore issues of science and society, Shakespeare delves into politics and morality. Forum Theatre enables young people to engage deeply with issues that concern them.

Ref 6
p 106

Moving on

How you end your time at school, whether nursery, primary or secondary, as a pupil, parent or teacher, is as significant as how you start. It deserves as just as much attention. One crucial issue for pupils is whether they leave as a valued citizen, a whole person capable of contributing to society whatever their academic achievement, or whether the sum of their existence is just an examination rank, however high. Learning takes many forms, and the modern world wants people skilled at caring, making and repairing things as well as academic abilities. Each child needs to celebrate the whole of their achievement on leaving school, as well as identify areas for further development.

In a citizenship school, the last year or two is increasingly concerned with transition to the next stage. In addition to work for assessment, this should include:
■ Peer preparation: training or supporting pupils starting school, through induction, peer mentoring, giving responsibilities;
■ Critical reflection: evaluating their own participation in school life;
■ Critical feedback: evaluating the school's performance, through focus groups, questionnaires, essays, an exhibition or other activity;
■ Peak performances: a production of some kind, in the arts, sport, entertainment, environment or community service, where each child can excel; and
■ Celebration, including a ceremony and a party, festival or fair.
■ In secondary school, 'citizenship placements' and preparation for active participation in democratic society should be as important as careers education and work placements.

Finally, a citizenship school will value its relationships with former pupils. Its achievement is not just measured by annual league tables, but by the lifelong contribution of its pupils to society. Former pupils can play an important part by returning to share their experiences, about good times and hard times, raising children and earning a living, making their mark or failing in life. Visits from past pupils, and not just the returning heroes, gives the whole school a sense of continuity and tangible feedback which helps motivate both pupils and teachers. When pupils go on to become parents, plumbers, nurses, community activists or entrepreneurs, and then choose to give something back to their school, it is a powerful sign that the school is doing something right.

Over time, the culture of a citizenship school will make a powerful contribution to the whole community. Its former pupils will become active and effective citizens, enriching society in many different ways.

Part 2: Learning freedom: the empowering classroom and curriculum

> **The child shall have the right to freedom of expression, including freedom to seek, receive and impart information and ideas of all kinds, regardless of frontiers, in any medium of the child's choice.**
>
> *Article 13, UN Convention on the Rights of the Child*

Citizenship across the curriculum

Citizenship can enrich the whole curriculum through democratic teaching methods as well as bringing out the social and ethical dimensions in all subjects. Good teaching inspires young people to learn and understand subjects in relation to life and the world. This kind of teaching requires teachers to be enthusiastic about their subject, interested in its wider relevance and committed to each individual student. This chapter is therefore as much about teaching any subject as about teaching citizenship, because the methods described are about sharing power in the classroom in constructive and positive ways.

At present, many pupils do not feel empowered by school. A recent study of 2,272 seven to seventeen year olds reported that only a quarter thought their teachers took their opinions seriously, and many were angered by the way teachers dismissed and mistrusted their views. In the Campaign for Learning survey by MORI of 3,000 eleven to sixteen year olds, pupils said their top three classroom activities were copying from the board or a book (56%) and listening to the teacher talk for a long time (37%) and classroom discussion (37%). They also ranked the first two activities among the least likely to help them learn better. Top of the list of activities most likely to help them learn was work on a computer (33%), work in a small group to solve a problem (33%) and have a class discussion (28%). Students who are able to develop their own views, who are taken seriously by teachers and are encouraged to pursue their own passions through learning, are likely to become both better students and more capable adults.

This means learning for one's own purposes as a free citizen, not for someone else. John Holt points out that learning is not a product of teaching: 'Learners create learning.'[24] Teachers can stimulate and encourage, but cannot make someone learn. Children learn rapidly when they want to, even without teachers. Children who 'buy into' the school's goals do well, but those who do not spend every single day struggling with something they do not want to do. They pursue private goals, ignoring, subverting or resisting the school agenda. Teaching in these circumstances is a permanent struggle. The struggle is even greater if teachers themselves are not sold on the curriculum.

> *Within a school framework which also promotes the social, moral and cultural development of pupils, [citizenship] promotes their personal and social development, enabling them to become more self-confident and responsible in and beyond the classroom.*
> **QCA National Curriculum for Citizenship**

While some schools may prefer to select pupils willing to learn, a citizenship school accepts everyone entitled to attend, just as a state cannot choose its citizens nor parents their children. The citizenship school starts from the needs and desire of its members, not the requirements of the school as an institution.

This brings us back to the tension at the heart of government policy. The national curriculum expresses an official consensus on what the state believes every child needs to learn to do well. But for many pupils this may be very different from what they want to know. A subject-based national curriculum may also fail to develop the six key skills sought by employers (communication, working with others, application of number, information technology, improving own learning and performance, problem solving) If used well, the national curriculum can raise aspirations and opportunities. But if imposed, a set curriculum stifles 'the holy curiosity of inquiry', as Einstein put it.[25]

This tension is an inescapable part of citizenship: we are born into a world we did not choose, with language, laws and institutions created by others, and as citizens we use our talents to adopt, adapt or alter these preconditions. The contradictions of a national curriculum can therefore be a challenge for creativity rather than an obstacle.

In practical terms, this means infusing the whole curriculum with the principles and practices of citizenship, so that the national curriculum is just one of many realities to be negotiated. While the teacher may 'cover' the curriculum, learners must discover it for themselves. That is, they do not really know it until they make it their own. This is as true for didactic instruction as for 'discovery learning'.

The citizenship school curriculum therefore recognises each individual pupil and their identity, needs and wants as the centre of their own learning. If these are ignored, teachers and pupils will be engaged in a constant struggle over each child's fundamental needs as a person. Although teachers may win the classroom battle, hearts and minds may be lost forever.

The bottom line is, if pupils lack a sense of power over their own learning as members of the school community, why should they believe anything in the citizenship curriculum? And if they dismiss citizenship education as a sham, it may simply add to the cynicism about politics and participation in public life.

These issues are also recognised in the curriculum for PSHE and citizenship, which aim to develop pupils':
■ confidence and responsibility and making the most of their abilities;
■ relationships and respect for differences between people;
■ skills of participation and action.

Developing these abilities are fundamentally about process. They cannot be learned except through experiences which engage each pupil's thinking, feeling and doing as a whole person in the world. In other words, simulated action in the classroom is not enough. A child may develop self-esteem and confidence in class, but get emotionally crushed at home or by other children away from school. A young person may create a stunning project at school, but lack the ability to transfer their skills into life beyond school. To be effective, citizenship education has to engage pupils as people living in particular social circumstances which they can influence as citizens. This presents teachers with considerable challenges. For one thing, teachers cannot do it alone. They have to involve other members of the community. But this challenge can also make teaching more empowering, enjoyable and stimulating.

For every age group, in every subject and every class, this means respecting each pupil's sense of self as a learner in a world they know best. The teacher's task is to widen their horizons and stretch their skills, but if adults do not respect the child's own world and sense of self, the child gets lost.

The diagram on page 63 illustrates the relationship between soft skills, like self-esteem and motivation, 'hard' skills and knowledge, and the social environment needed to sustain high achievement. Although this applies to all learning, the distinctive feature of a citizenship school is that the social environment is not run by one group of people (managers, teachers) in order to make another group (pupils, teachers) produce high results, but that all groups share the power and responsibility to create their social environment.

In summary the fundamental elements of an empowering curriculum are:
1. Developing a sense of self as a person, learner and agent in the world;

Learning freedom: the empowering classroom and curriculum

2. Partnership with parents;
3. Sharing responsibility for learning;
4. Clarifying values and virtues;
5. Learning to learn;
6. Emotional literacy and understanding feelings;
7. Thinking skills, applied to real as well as hypothetical and historical problems;
8. Inquiry and research skills, testing ideas against evidence;
9. Communication skills, including listening, drawing, writing and discussing;
10. Skills of participation and action, including team-work, negotiating, decision-making and planning;
11. Acquiring socially powerful knowledge;
12. Self-assessment and evaluation the work of others.

These aspects of an empowering curriculum are a fuller version of the learning cycle and cover many of the skills in the citizenship curriculum. This Chapter describes each of these in more detail.

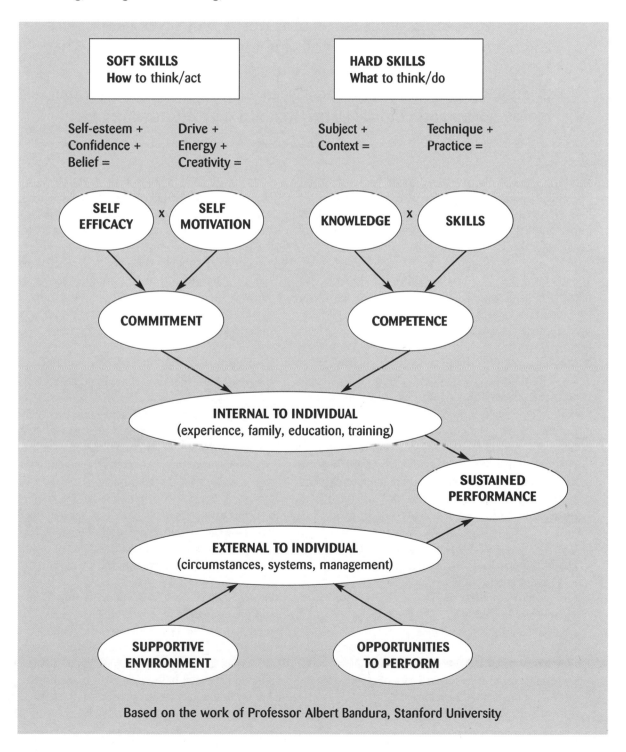

Based on the work of Professor Albert Bandura, Stanford University

Developing a sense of self

Citizenship is stunted without a sense of self and power as a person. If you lack a sense of your self and own intrinsic value as a person, it is difficult to be an independent learner or member of society, because you depend on others' approval, direction or instructions.

However, the main activity of schools is to give children instructions, direction and approval (or disapproval) in how to follow a curriculum and regime set by others. It is very difficult to develop a sense of self as one person in a class of thirty, following a daily timetable of tasks planned by others, constantly supervised by adults, with little

Developing a sense of purpose and personal worth

Pupils 'learn to recognise their own worth, work well with others and become increasingly responsible for their own learning. They reflect on their experiences and understand how they are developing personally and socially, tackling many of the spiritual, moral, social and cultural issues that are part of growing up.'

Preamble, National Curriculum on PSHE and Citizenship

Enabling students to develop a sense of purpose is a foundation for learning and citizenship as well life. It is also required under Attainment Target 1 of the non-statutory guidelines for personal, social and health education.

The following activities can be done in Circle Time, form time or PSHE lessons. They need to be done sensitively, with regard to each pupil's age, circumstances and their right to privacy about their personal lives.

● **Sharing circle:** Invite pupils to bring something personal from home, to share and talk about in pairs and with the class. This activity can continue over a month, by inviting one or two children every day to describe their object in more depth. This must be done with sensitivity, with preparation to ensure that children appreciate and respect each other. There has to be enough time to explore personal meanings and differences. This activity can be part of an induction process for a new intake.

● Give each student a private **Personal Goals Book** or Learning Journal and encourage them to identify goals in different areas, such as:
 • things they want to do with friends
 • family and home life
 • skills and subjects at school
 • diet, health and physical activities, including sport
 • artistic, cultural and creative activities
 • interests or hobbies outside school
 • personal or spiritual development
 • travel or longer breaks

 • service to others and the environment
This works best when treated as a private activity, not as part of a public Record of Achievement, which pupils can choose to show other pupils or teachers if they wish.

● Encourage students to list and review their own goals at the start and end of each month, term and year, in private, but as part of school time. Suggest that students might like to discuss these goals with friends, parents or other family members.

● Set up a peer-support and/or mentoring system to support students developing their personal goals.

● Invite parents, local celebrities and other members of the community into school to discuss goals they had when they were young, what happened and how they came to make the life choices they did.

Show that keeping Personal Goals Book or Learning Journal is a valuable activity by making time for it at the end of the day or during the week, but always protect its privacy as a personal activity for pupils to develop their own sense of direction and purpose.

Careers' education is a particularly important time to help young people focus on their life goals, but the inspiration for what they want to do can come through any subject or anything in the world. There are many books and courses on developing personal goals, usually found on the self-help shelves of bookshops. Many of these can be adapted for school use. Teachers may also find them useful!

Ref 8
p 108

Learning freedom: the empowering classroom and curriculum

individual attention and treated mainly as a member of a group.

Circle time and other activities, outlined elsewhere in this book, can help to develop a sense of self. But there are a few essential preconditions. The following simple actions help people develop positive self esteem in school:

- **unconditional acceptance:** this means recognising and greeting each person by name, acknowledging them in a positive way, not putting them down, and showing that their experiences, culture, language and background are accepted;
- **sense of purpose:** enabling young people to express and develop their own goals as people, so that they are not defined exclusively as pupils;
- **safety:** building emotional and physical safety through consistent boundaries;
- **identity:** allowing young people to say how they wish to be identified and recognised;
- **sense of power and achievement:** giving people opportunities to succeed at something and to make a difference and have an impact, and to show that they can influence events;
- **feedback:** focused, honest feedback on what they do, both positive and negative: this means separating comments about what they do from who they are.

If children (or adults) do not get this kind of support, they will often develop a sense of self by drawing attention to themselves through negative or destructive behaviour. They may even define themselves in negative terms and then provoke reactions which confirm negative beliefs about themselves.

There are now many self-esteem programmes and activities to develop these qualities in school. Alistair Smith uses the acronym BASIC, Belonging, Aspirations, Safety, Identity and Success to help remember them.

Ref 7 p 107

Partnership with parents

Children form many of their fundamental behaviours and beliefs about citizenship through their experiences at home. All families are a social microcosm, each with its own ways of making and enforcing rules, rewarding or punishing behaviour, allocating resources, coping with the environment and providing a shared framework for its members. Children learn about authority, power, justice, decision-

making and many other aspects of citizenship through family relationships. What they learn depends on their particular family.

Schools need to involve parents in citizenship education, as with other areas of the curriculum. Almost all parents have something to contribute to the curriculum, but particular sensitivity is necessary with citizenship. Some parents have strong views on certain issues. Treated with sensitivity and respect, different views can bring a variety of perspectives to citizenship at school. Parents involved in the school, local community or wider world can be particularly helpful in extending the school curriculum.

Citizenship education at school can also contribute to family life. The United Nations International Year of the Family in 1994 had the slogan, "Building the smallest democracy at the heart of society". The citizenship curriculum and Rights of the Child could have profound implications for family life. Families are one of society's most violent institutions. People are more likely to be hit, beaten or killed in their own homes by other family members than anywhere else.[26] Domestic violence is the second most common type of violent crime reported to the police, a quarter of all reported violent crime.[27] Most children are hit by their parents[28] and some sixty per cent of under-18 homicide victims were killed by their parents, compared with less than a fifth by strangers.[29] Studies of violence in families also show that 'democratic households' - where decision-making is shared - are the least violent. Homes where all decisions are made by either parent have the highest rates of violence.[30]

Family issues such as unhappiness, neglect, violence or sexual abuse are likely to arise when feelings are discussed at school. This can happen at any age, for adults as well as children. Staff need to be able to respond in a supportive and appropriate way.

Partnership with parents as a child's first and most enduring educator is increasingly recognised as essential for achievement at school. Children start learning from birth and schools can do a great deal to encourage parents to help children learn, take part in parenting courses and develop positive relationships as a child's first educator. Peers secondary school in Oxford, for example, runs courses for pre-school children and their parents on the premises. Growing numbers of primary and secondary schools are running courses for parents in accelerated learning, computing, using the internet, learning to learn and thinking skills, as well as conventional schools subjects.

Ref 9
p 109

Home life is the inescapable foundation for learning for any child, and the better schools are able to work in partnership with parents and carers, the more children can develop a sense of self worth, of the importance of learning, and the freedom to learn.

Sharing responsibility for learning

One of the simplest and most effective ways of empowering pupils is to give them responsibility for planning and assessment of learning. Children are natural learners. They observe, figure out what is going on and act accordingly. Even slow learners work out pretty fast what is going on. When they realise they are playing a game they cannot win they create a game they can, which might be playing dumb, playing up or playing the bully, according to their talents. And if they cannot make sense of the world, they become disturbed. Difficult behaviour is often an appeal for help. Difficult pupils are, in effect, using the only power they have – the ability to disrupt - to assert their needs.

> *Any teaching that the learner has not asked for is likely to impede and prevent his or her learning.*
> **John Holt, Learning All the Time**[31]

All skills and knowledge have many purposes - for the individual, for society, and for the subject itself as an evolving discipline. One person's pleasure and interest in a subject may be quite different from its function in society. But people learn best when they are passionate about something or their lives depend on it. Then they really want to know. Kindling a personal interest in a subject means making connections with the learners' purposes and those of the subject on as many different levels as possible.

At a time when the amount that could be learnt is much greater than any person could

possibly know, the ability to decide for oneself what is important and worth knowing is more important than learning whatever one is told to learn. Every course must therefore include an exploration of the purpose and values of the subject in order to enable young people to make these decisions for themselves.

Enabling young people to identify their own purpose for studying a subject will increase motivation and helps to develop the essential skills of self-directed learning.

The High Scope model of 'plan, do, review' provides a simple but powerful tool for learning which can help children organise their learning. At the start of every year, term, module, week, day or topic, ask children what they want to learn and how they want to learn it. As we have a national curriculum, which reflects a professional and political agreement of what is to be learnt, teachers also have a responsibility to ensure that children learn certain topics. The teacher's task is to make this enticing. Then at then end of every topic, day, week, module, term and year, learners need to review what they have done. The details of teaching and learning styles are beyond the scope of this book, but the following sections illustrate different ways of bringing the practice of citizenship into everyday teaching.

Sharing responsibility for learning: co-planning the curriculum

Learning citizenship is an active process that must be embedded in everyday classroom practices if it is to win young people's respect and participation. This means sharing responsibility for learning, so that teachers involve young people in planning their own learning as far as possible. Some of the best examples of this are in the early years, as in High Scope. In secondary schools there are many good examples in project learning, PSHE, TVEI or work experience programmes.

Shared Learning in Action is an approach to empowering young people to address issues that concern them. The programme is used mainly in PSHE and has covered issues such as bullying, crime prevention, drugs, environment, food choices, safety and transport, but the approach can be adapted to other subjects. The central features of Shared Learning in Action (SLA) are that young people set the agenda, work in groups and take action to

Learning freedom: the empowering classroom and curriculum

Shared learning in practice

Early Years

At Newall Green Nursery and Infant School in Manchester, nursery children plan their day with their parents. "At the beginning of the day each child chooses five activities. The activities are represented by picture cards which children stick on a wall chart under their name. Parents help their children to record their choices on individual charts which become a personal record. At this time parents can encourage children to try new or different activities so that they have a broad and balanced experience across the curriculum. During the day, as the children complete each chosen activity, they remove the picture from the wall chart and return it to the box provided." At the end of the day, parents talk with their children about what they have done during the day.[32]

Primary

Gordon Wells describes an inner London primary school teacher who gave each pupil a 'choice book', a learning diary in which the agenda of tasks to be completed is negotiated once a week. At the start of the year the agenda consisted largely of tasks suggested by the teacher, but over time the child adds more of their own suggestions. They evaluated their tasks and make suggestions for how they could improve. The teacher gives specific feedback and suggests new activities.[33]

Secondary:

At Peers School in Oxford "you have a go at everything" in the first year. "After that you get a choice and you can change your mind as you go along - so you don't have to plan your life at thirteen and make too many decisions." (Keith) "In science it's divided into different units so you can concentrate on one bit at a time. You're not forced into anything you don't want to do." (Jane) "When you file your work you can see it building up. You can be proud of it and its something you can take and show people. You can look back on it and improve on your faults." (Keith)

Peers has a modular programme divided into units or credits. This helps pupils and teachers to structure courses, and gives students clear objectives to aim at over a short period of time. Students have more frequent choices about what credits they will take as the course develops. This improves motivation and sustains interest.[34]

make a difference. Trained adults provide a clear structure and support.

The seven steps in Shared Learning in Action are:

1. **Understanding feelings:** a structured sequence of activities to help children explore emotions, empathy, what affects feelings and how they influence behaviour.
2. **Identify issues and make a list:** activities to acknowledge prior knowledge.
3. **Select and prioritise** issues from the list and form project groups.
4. **Research:** groups find out information on the topic, from other people as well as other sources.
5. **Share and decide:** groups present their findings to each other and decide what they can do about the issues explored.
6. **Take action:** activities vary from presenting ideas through drama and song, to writing letters to MPs or counsellors, to practical projects like Positive Lunchtimes (see p 73).
7. **Review:** children discuss their degrees of success, difficulties that arose and what can be learnt from the experience.

This cycle of activities is very close to that advocated in this book, appreciative inquiry (p 71) and Changemakers. Training and materials are available.

Ref 18
p 112

Sharing responsibility for learning: Gaining an overview of the subject

Children sometimes have only the haziest idea of what they are learning and why. Although it is impossible to know everything about a subject, or even a small topic within it, it is possible to know what a subject is about and why it matters before going into it in detail. It is often this sense of a subject which motivates people to find out more. Seeing any topic or subject as a whole is therefore a crucial part of becoming a 'learning citizen'.

Different people find different routes into subjects, so there are many ways of giving pupils an overview, which can be adapted according to age and subject. What matters is that every course, every term and every lesson starts by considering the purpose, context and overview of what is to be learnt. This process is like winding up a clock or recharging a battery - it can seem like a delay, but once it is done you go faster and farther.

There at several ways in which a whole topic or subject can be seen, including:

■ as a discipline or body of ideas and skills;
■ in a social context, as something which has meaning and purpose in the world;
■ in terms of their own lives.

Finding out and recognising pupils' prior knowledge treats them as active learners, rather than recipients of knowledge, and including them in planning the curriculum. After conducting an exercise, like one of those below, teachers can discuss with pupils what order they would like to tackle the subject, what aspects need more time, and what can be done more quickly, who might need extra help and who would be willing to help other children learn. This discussion shifts the focus from playing the game of getting by in class to learning for oneself and helping others learn. It can also be used to create an outline lesson plan for the subject for the term ahead. Both of these activities are essential aspects of learning citizenship.

Sharing responsibilities for learning

The following exercises can be done with pupils when starting work on a new subject or topic. Results from these exercises can be displayed in the classroom during the course, as a reference point. In many cases it is worth repeating the exercise at the end of the course, remove the display.

Brainstorming: Divide the class into mixed ability groups of five or six pupils ('learning teams') and ask each group to brainstorm what they know about the subject for 10-15 minutes (or longer if appropriate). Ask each group to report two or three things to the whole class, so that there is a shared sense of where the class is starting.

Valuing the subject: Ask each group to come up with reasons why the subject or topic is worth studying. After each group has a list of reasons, pool them on a single list for the whole class and discuss different kinds of reason, such as – utility, enjoyment, intrinsic/for its own sake. After pupils have had a full discussion, the teacher can suggest other reasons, invite a specialist speaker or visit a place where the subject is used to increase insight and motivation.

Prioritising: Pupils could be asked to prioritise reasons for studying a topic or to prioritise topics within a subject. Either way, this is an elementary exercise of democracy in action which engages pupils in the subject and tells the teacher what they think about it. Prioritisation can be done in several ways: asking for a show of hands against each item on the list; holding a ballot; giving everyone three sticky dots to put against their three top priorities; asking each group to do a card sort (putting the reasons on cards and sorting them in order).

Curriculum card sort: there are many variations of this useful exercise. Each of the main topics to be covered is written on a separate, numbered card. Children work in groups of about six, taking turns to read the subject on a card. The group then discusses what they know about the topic and decide which of three piles to put it on - A: know nothing, B: know something, C: know a lot.

If teachers want to know more about individual levels of knowledge, they could first run through the list of topics as a quiz, so that each child notes the number on a personal topic sheet and writes A, B or C against it, where A= know nothing, B= know something, C= know a lot. It is important that there is no shame in not knowing anything about the topic – after all, it has not yet been taught.

After all the cards have been put into piles, each group says how many cards are on each pile. The teacher can then ask one child in each group to pick a card from the C pile and say something about the topic.

This game raises awareness of the topics to be covered and gives the teacher an idea about current knowledge. Personal topic sheets from each child give more detailed information about what each child thinks they know about the topic. This information can be used to construct peer education pairs or groups within the class.

As a separate exercise, or as a continuation of the above, each group of children is asked to place the card on the table in relation to other topics, like a domino board, creating a visual map of the subject. Children can also be asked to discuss what order they would like to study the topics. (See page 8 for an example card sort for the purpose of education).

Topic bingo: Give each pupil a bingo style sheet with random numbers, corresponding to topics in the subject. The teacher (or a pupil) reads out the number and the topic. If pupils know something about it, they cross off the number. The first pupil to cross of a row of two, three, four or five has to show that they know something about each of the topics by telling the whole class.

Quiz show: This is similar to the above, except that pupils work in groups of four or five.

Draw a picture of the subject: ask each pupil to draw a picture illustrating what he or she knows about a subject. Emphasise that the quality of the picture is less important than what they draw (although obviously good drawings should be encouraged and welcomed). This makes it possible for children who have difficulty writing to take part. Then ask each child to describe the subject to a small group of other children and as a group to identify what they do and do not know about the subject. The teacher should listen in to the groups, particularly when children who have difficulty learning are describing what they know. Ask each group to report back what they know and do not know. Praise children for admitting that they do not know something - this helps to reduce anxiety and encourages children to take risks and thus be more open to learning.

Pictures can be collected in at the end of the session and used to assess starting points. Repeat the exercise at the end of the course and let children compare pictures to see progress. Display all the pictures, or the best, or most interesting – or ask pupils to choose which to display.

Concept mapping: ask pupils to discuss in pairs what they know about a subject, then in groups or as a class draw a 'concept mind' of the main ideas and facts, for example see illustration page 21

Philosophical enquiry: tell pupils something about the subject – what it is about, the main ideas, knowledge and skills involved, without going into any detail – then give them time to think of questions about it. If they are unfamiliar with asking questions, give two or three examples of the kinds of questions that intrigue you about it, or practice using a topic they all know about. Pupils can be asked to discuss questions in small groups, so that each group chooses two or three questions, or the questions can be pooled as a whole class. All the questions are written up on the board and then everyone votes for one question to discuss. This will lead to a list of questions in priority order, chosen by pupils, which can then be used to structure the curriculum.

Display: use posters illustrating the aims, main ideas, pioneering figures and uses of a subject, including the best materials produced by previous years.

Story telling and retelling: telling a story is one of the most effective ways of drawing children into a subject. Story is one of our primordial ways of recalling and transmitting experience, from ancient myths and the bible to Shakespeare and soap opera. All knowledge is rich with stories and characters - Pythagoras, Galileo, the discovery of DNA, the invention of the internet and thousands more. Most people remember stories, events and characters better than abstract facts. *Teaching as Story Telling* by Kieran Egan[35] shows how to engage children's imagination through the form of a story. This is not about using fictional stories, but how the story form can be used to plan lessons and topics. Story is also one of the ways people put themselves into the plot of life as learning citizens. Aspiring artists, mathematicians, politicians or scientists are as likely to be inspired by the stories of heroes and innovators in the field as the subject matter itself.

Subject scrap book: keep a scrap book of illustrations, stories and pupil's work on each subject, so that pupils have a sense of contributing to a growing body of knowledge within the class. The book can either remain with one group of students as they move through the school or can remain with each year, so that later years can add to it.

A model environment: The most powerful way of giving pupils an overview of the subject is to immerse them in it. This can be done by visiting and spending time in a relevant environment, or by creating it in the school or grounds. A junior school in Rochdale has a large open plan classroom laid out like streets with stalls, shops and local services. These are used for a wide variety of hands-on learning activities. Many schools have created nature areas as an 'outdoor classroom'.

Visits: when embarking on a subject, organise an appropriate visit to a museum, theatre, film, work place or agency, to see how the subject is used in the world.

Guest speakers: invite speakers who use the subject in their lives to talk about it and answer questions.

Sharing responsibility for learning: learning beyond school

Education out of school is at last being recognised as an essential part of the education system and it provides many more opportunities for young people to take responsibility for their own learning and to develop skills and knowledge in citizenship. Between the ages of 5 and 16, children spend less than a third of waking time in school, often as little as a quarter. Most children spend more time watching television than in class. The challenge for our society, not just schools, is to create varied opportunities for learning that engage, challenge and empower young people to become active learning citizens.

Schools can support this by:
- encouraging parents to do things with their children;
- create time, space and resources for children to pursue their own learning interests;
- organising study support, extra-curricular activities and clubs;
- making facilities available to community organisations;
- involving pupils in local organisations through placements, projects and community service;
- building active links with libraries, museums and 'centres of curiosity and imagination';
- organising field trips and visits to places of interest;
- residential programmes and exchanges; and
- setting up holiday programmes, of activities to take home, play schemes and summer schools.

Ref 10
p 109

All of these activities create opportunities for young people to organise their own learning and to take responsibility for an aspect of each event, as part of a team.

Learning values and virtues

Pupils learn 'about the key concepts, values or dispositions of fairness, social justice, respect for democracy and diversity; through study which covers issues at a range of levels, for example, school, local, national, global; and through learning in the community.'
QCA Programmes of study for Citizenship

All learning assumes a purpose, which is often unspoken. As argued in Chapter Five, values answer the question 'why?', often at a fundamental level (see p 47). The purpose of traditional school learning is decided by authority - the teacher, school, religion (sometimes), Qualifications and Curriculum Authority (QCA) or government. In a citizenship school, learners themselves develop the capacity to answer the question 'why?', in relation to life as well as each subject.

A citizenship school clearly aims to live by core virtues such as 'fairness, social justice, respect for democracy and diversity', as set out in the national curriculum for citizenship. This means enabling pupils to understand the complex layers of authority in society and develop their own authority as citizens so

that they can decide the purpose of their own learning. This makes it particularly important for pupils to understand and develop their own inner code of values, as well as the values underlying the school and their subjects

There are broadly three strands of learning values in education, including:
- transmitting deeply held beliefs (virtues) of a culture, society, institution or religion;
- understanding different value systems, including the values of every subject; and
- values clarification, or helping people clarify and develop their own values.

Children have a right to think what they like and be whatever religion they want to be.
Article 14, UN Convention on the Rights of the Child

These need not be incompatible. Every society, faith and institution lives by certain virtues, which may be spelt out through codes of conduct, rules, role models, sayings and stories, or may be implicit in the way things are done. The Universal Declaration of Human Rights, the Rights of the Child and citizenship values of 'fairness, social justice, respect for democracy and diversity' are part of the values our government is pledged to transmit. Understanding different value systems is often the subject of religious education, but every subject has its own values, such as objectivity and recourse to experience in science, empathy in literature or competition and cooperation in sports. Values clarification is the process through which people clarify and develop distinct values of their own. The materials listed cover all three strands.

Ref 11
p 109

Emotional literacy

Emotions are a powerful dimension of politics and community action, although they are more explicit in the curriculum for PSHE than for citizenship. The Healthy Schools Initiative is strongly informed by the importance of emotions for personal well-being and learning. Citizenship schools aim to bring these different strands together in a consistent way, so that these different dimensions of learning support each other.

The ability to understand, interpret and deal with emotions is increasingly recognised as

Learning freedom: the empowering classroom and curriculum

fundamental for effective learning. The publication of *Emotional Intelligence* by Daniel Goleman[36] brought together evidence from studies of the brain and learning to demonstrate the role of emotions for education and life. The book also outlines several education programmes on emotional literacy, to which new courses are being added all the time. In fact the whole body is involved in learning, as demonstrated by neurophysiologist and educator Carla Hannaford.

Ref 12
p 110

Learning to learn

Study skills are fundamental to becoming a powerful 'learning citizen'. At pre-school, the High-Scope curriculum model of 'plan, do, review' can give children a profound experience of the learning cycle in practice. Long-term studies show that this model can contribute to significant gains in achievement throughout life.

There is considerable evidence that premature pressure on children to read and write at an early age can put them off learning later, while children who develop the capacity and joy of learning through play can learn to read rapidly when they are ready, often at about the age of 7 rather than 5 or 6.

The Campaign for Learning has launched a learning to learn action research project with 24 schools from nursery to sixth form, to explore and evaluate the best ways of giving pupils the understanding, skills and motivation to learn well.

Ref 13
p 110

Thinking skills

Independent, critical thinking is a core skill for citizenship and lifelong learning. There is now substantial experience of teaching thinking to children of all ages. *Philosophy with Children*, developed by Karen Muris, is an enjoyable approach for primary children between about 5 and 12, which encourages children to ask questions and then discuss them in depth. Lessons start by reading a picture story or showing a video to stimulate thinking. Children are then asked to pose questions about anything that seemed strange, puzzling or curious in the story, without answering the questions. After a period of thinking time, they decide together which questions to discuss. The development of the class as a 'community of inquiry' is central to the process. This approach draws on the work of Matthew Lipman, which was inspired by John Dewey and the Russian philosopher Vygotsky.[37] A growing variety of material and organisations are available to support teaching in thinking skills.

Ref 14
p 111

Enquiry and research skills

Learning involves testing ideas against evidence. In citizenship schools these skills are developed through the subject, pupil's own concerns, the school environment (see p 57) and school improvement.

Involving students in school improvement gives them practical experience of identifying and investigating a problem, formulating proposals and presenting them to others. It also takes their views seriously and provides the school with low-cost consultancy that can be more penetrating and effective than expensive outsiders.

There are many different models of investigation by pupils, depending on their age and the subject. Appreciative inquiry uses a framework of questions to get an in depth understanding about people's views. Changemakers (p 112), Learning through Landscapes and Shared Learning in Action (p 66), see also Positive Lunchtimes, (p 73) also offer pupils practical ways of improving the school through action research. Students as Researchers is a model developed by a Bedfordshire comprehensive school and the University of Cambridge Education Department, described in the box on page 72.

Appreciative inquiry

Appreciative Inquiry is an approach to change that stimulates people involved in an issue to develop positive solutions. Instead of focusing on the problem, it looks at what is working in order to build on success. At its simplest, it means asking after a meeting or event 'What worked?' 'What did we do well?' The aim is to notice what works and to do more of it.

Since 1992, it has been used by young, disadvantaged people in Chicago to bring about change in the city through a project called Imagine Chicago. Pairs of young people interviewed people in key positions throughout the city, from the mayor and police chief to

Students as partners in school improvement

Sharnbrook Upper School and Community College has 1,600 pupils with a relatively high level of pupil involvement. Every curriculum area has a teacher responsible for increasing pupil involvement. With support from the University of Cambridge School of Education, the school has developed a rigorous approach to student-led research as a contribution to school improvement.

Groups of about 15 students from Years 9 to 13, together with supporting members of staff, spend a day learning about research methods at the university. The students identify specific issues to investigate in small groups, with staff support. Issues covered are often critical, such as the conditions for students to have a voice, profiling and assessment, trainee teachers, school meals, careers education, life skills lessons, gender differences, post-16 choices or social space for students. Having identified an issue, the students clarify the key questions, through discussion and pilot studies. The specific questions are then investigated through questionnaires or other methods. The students then evaluate the evidence, draw conclusions and make recommendations which are presented to appropriate forums.

Many of the students' recommendations have been implemented. For example, the study of school meals lead to more variety and choice on the menu. The tutorial and life skills programme was fundamentally changed to a negotiated curriculum with input from a panel of specialist tutors, external speakers and students who have personal knowledge of the issues being discussed. The central recommendation was that "Students should be the driving force behind life skills lessons." The students' proposals for trainee teachers took three years to implement, but now all trainee teachers get feedback on their lessons from students.

For students the project has increased team work across years, developed confidence, made them feel valued members of the school and developed their understanding of how the school works. "It has given me the skills and confidence to state my point of view more firmly to the point where I am able to argue points with teachers outside Students as Researchers meetings" said one. Students have also learned how to do surveys and work with the school system to bring about evidence-based change. "You learn to accept that not everybody has the same views as you for the partnership to succeed... but that controversy may be the motivation the group needs."

As a result of the project, the school has also included three students on the group monitoring and evaluating the impact of changes to the curriculum.

A key factor for the success of the project is the trust and support of staff. Other important factors include having a decent chunk of time for students to work together, regular meetings in dedicated time, and the support of an experienced, empathetic researcher.

Ref 15
p 111

teachers, youth workers and wardens. Information was used to develop civic projects that create a positive future for themselves and the city. This is not an 'objective' survey, because any inquiry influences its subject and appreciative inquiry aims to raise spirits as well as involve people in creating imaginative solutions. This approach is ideal for pupils to use, but it is best if a cross-section of the school community is involved.

It follows a few simple steps:
1. Choose a topic: what we focus on gets magnified by our attention, so choose an issue worth magnifying.
2. Develop questions: questions should explore what works, what people value and positive experiences in relation to the topic, and then what made it possible, when and why it worked.

3. Test run: try the questions out on each other and a few other people first.
4. Ask questions: in pairs, interview a broad sample of people involved in the topic, and note the replies. Encourage interviewees to tell stories, give examples and anecdotes. This can raise a lot of negative feelings and opinions, so it is important to keep coming back to things that worked. Where there is a lot of negativity, ask what would make a difference, how could it be turned round, and have they ever been in a similar or equivalent situation which was positive?
5. Share information: get all pairs to share information, starting with the most exciting, interesting stories and 'quotable quotes'.
6. Identify themes: see if any common themes emerge from the different stories.
7. Write a 'provocative proposition': this is a positive statement that describes an idealised

future as if it is already happening, incorporating all the common themes. Provocative propositions are intended to stretch and challenge, based on the best of what exists.

The aim of Appreciative Inquiry is to distil the best out of people's experiences and create a vision or ideal to aim for. The process touches something important in people, so they give heartfelt answers. It has to be conducted with respect for all involved. At its best it awakes in people aspirations to bring about changes for the better. In this sense it is the opposite of an Ofsted inspection.

Almost any topics is suitable for appreciative inquiry - assemblies, breaks, form time, induction of new parents and pupils, the play ground, work with parents or establishing the aims of the school.

Ref 14 p 111

If an appreciative inquiry is conducted, it is important that the information is acted on.

Peer education

The best way of learning something is to teach it.

Peer education means learners helping each other by teaching. Young people love the responsibility of teaching, and the pupils being taught get more attention by working one-to-one or in small groups. Peer education is used in many different ways - with children teaching others in the same class, older pupils teaching younger ones in the same school, secondary students teaching primary pupils, college students teaching secondary or primary pupils, parents running courses for other parents. In most cases a professional educator organises, trains and supports lay (non-professional) teachers who are relatively close in age, ability and position to the people they teach. This is different from mentoring, where mentors are older and more experienced (see following section).

For example, IBIS Trust worked with Misbourne school in Buckinghamshire to train sixth form students. The young people identified drug usage as a topic they wanted to work on. The Trust ran a series of needs assessment sessions with staff and students, and the students drew up a detailed brief of the training and support they wanted. The project drew on local agencies for support, who provided input on drug use and minimisation, support services, first aid and advocacy. The Trust provided training in peer education skills, activities and techniques through the PEERAID materials (see Resources). The programme was run for Year 8 pupils, who responded positively. "I have learnt so much ... and it's been loads of fun!"

Peer education makes learning more efficient, effective and pleasurable for those who are taught, because they get more attention within a small group, as well as increasing the learning of the peer educators themselves. Used by pupils in school, it can give everyone a shared responsibility and understanding of teaching. Far from eroding respect for the craft of teaching, peer education increases it.

A citizenship school ensures that at some stage every pupil has responsibility for teaching others, one-to-one or in small groups, for at least a term, if not for most of their time at the school. This can take various forms, according to the needs and circumstances of the school:

■ **Learning partners** (see p 82) or **co-tutoring** where pairs of pupils support each other.
■ **Proctoring,** where more advanced pupils help others follow the work by asking and answering questions and give feedback.
■ **Paired reading** between pupils of different abilities or age groups.
■ **Peer support** systems aim to enhance the

Positive Lunchtimes

Positive Lunchtimes is a project developed by Year 6 pupils in several schools using the Shared Learning in Action approach (see p 66). Pupils in each school identified problems with the lunch breaks and decided what to do about them. One group devised a schedule of games to play with younger pupils for the playground and wet breaks. At another school children felt that playground activities were limited to boys playing football, so they bought skipping ropes, small balls, bean bags and other equipment and started a programme to bring about a fairer use of play space. In another school pupils felt that meals were too rushed, so they set up a rota for lunch sittings. An accredited training programme has also been set up for lunchtime assistants as a result of pupils' concerns.

social and emotional well-being in schools by enabling student to offer help to fellow students, such as listening, befriending or education projects.

■ **Learning carousel or jigsaw:** divide the class into equal sized groups (or learning teams) of four, five or six pupils. Team members each take a number from 1 to 6 or however many are in the group, and then all 1s, 2s, 3s etc form a new group to study one part of a topic or subject together. The teams then reform and pupils take turns to teach other members of the team their part of the subject. This technique works best with a narrative, as in English or history where children have an incentive to learn from each other to get the whole story, or where different topics add up to a whole picture, as in biology or geography. It also depends on having subject matter that is easy to learn from a book or other source in self-directed groups and easy to divide up into equally difficult tasks, although in a class of very mixed ability the numbering can be used to bring pupils of similar ability together, so that a group of slow pupils can be taught by the teacher and still make a contribution when they rejoin their learning team.

■ **Homework helpers,** where college or secondary school students are trained to tutor younger pupils having difficulty with their homework. Schemes like this have helped thousands of pupils in hundreds of schools in disadvantaged areas of New York.

**Ref 16
p 111**

Mentoring

Mentoring is a learning partnership between a more and a less experienced person. There is considerable evidence that active encouragement from a significant adult is one of the most powerful ways of giving young people belief in themselves, motivation to learn and resilience to face adversity. The word 'mentor' comes from the Greek advisor to Telemachus, son of Odysseus, with its root in Greek for 'to think'. A mentor is like a wise parent and guide, who performs an essential citizenship role by advising a young person through a long-term one-to-one relationship.

Mentors can help young people take control over their lives by creating a close relationship with an adult who
■ is independent of family or the school;

■ provides a sympathetic and mature sounding board;
■ offers advice and support;
■ gives additional insight into the adult world;
■ and can act as a role model.

Training and support for mentors is essential for schemes to work effectively. A trained mentor can help young people talk through different aspects of their lives, using what is known as the 'Five C' model - Challenges, Choices, Consequences, Creative Solutions and Conclusions.

**Ref 17
p 112**

Project learning, community enterprise and service learning

Citizenship 'encourages pupils to play a helpful part in the life of their schools, neighbourhoods, communities and the wider world.'
Preamble, National Curriculum for Citizenship

In a citizenship school people learn through doing as much as by study and reflection. All written material is the product of someone's learning. It can help others learn, but without some grounding in experience, people acquire the appearance of learning rather than its substance. In The Unschooled Mind, Howard Gardner[38] described top physics graduates at university who had fundamental misconceptions of core concepts in physics because they based their actual thinking on mental models developed in early childhood. Although they can use the concepts and powerful mathematics involved, they do not 'know' what they are doing with the powerful skills and knowledge they have acquired.

In a society where markets play an important and often powerful role in decision-making, it is essential for young people to understand how markets work and to learn relevant skills and abilities such as enterprise, negotiating and handling finance.

Community enterprise and project learning aim to ground education in experience. Although most science teaching includes experiments, they are often ritual repetitions of classic tests and training in technique rather then real investigations. Real experiments involve uncertainty as ideas are tested in practice. For traditional schools, working to a tight timetable with no room for trial and error, this is a major challenge.

The uncertainty of project learning can be reduced by
- training students in project development;
- ensuring that projects have achievable goals;
- carefully choosing or setting up projects within a clear framework;
- building in time for reflection and evaluation; and
- creating opportunities to assimilate and apply experience, skills and knowledge gained.

However, these helpful strategies can also undermine the powerful learning that can come from attempting the impossible, from failure or from struggling with a total lack of clarity. Allowing students to struggle in the dark, become disheartened by lack of progress or to reinvent the wheel is irresponsible, but if pupils are determined to take on a seemingly impossible challenge, it may be the greatest learning experience of their lives. The answer is to have skilled, experienced facilitators who can help pupils tackle projects in their own lives outside school as well as within the school and the curriculum.

Many pupils have projects in life, including hobbies, keeping pets, collecting, making things, helping the family or community activities. School can support pupils' own projects during induction to the school, circle time and extra-curricular activities. Pupils should feel able to bring problems to school and expect support in solving it, from a sympathetic ear to facilities and expert support.

Planned **project learning** within the curriculum includes:
- subject-based activities and projects, which may also involve home-learning, service learning or student responsibilities, such as calculating the energy efficiency of the school for a maths or science course;
- school conferences, project days or activity weeks;
- programmes such as Changemakers, Social Invention Workshops, Working for Myself or Community Enterprise; and
- commercial or charitable services to the school or its community.

Pupils (as well as parents or other adults) can be actively involved in running services that provide real benefits as well as learning opportunities. Pupils can run Tradecraft stalls, selling fairly traded tea, coffee and other goods, while learning about where they come from, how they are produced and global relationships. They can collect and refurbish tools, books or even computer equipment for developing countries.

Service learning is closer to volunteering, involving pupils in community projects. Community Service Volunteers (CSV) has pioneered support for service learning in Britain, particularly through its Lighthouse Schools Project

For example, pupils at Palatine High School in Blackpool use school equipment and a training package they have created to teach blind people in using the internet and information technology. Colne Valley High School in Huddersfield have set up a publishing project which produced a tourist guide book to the area that is widely sold. Pupils at Pensnett School in Brierley Hill, West Midlands, undertake childcare placements at local nurseries, while studying an accredited childcare course and producing learning packs for parents to use with their children at home. Pupils at St Benedict School in Derby work with a local rock musician and theatre group to take performances to primary schools. Projects like these are supported by Community Service Volunteers, which works with hundreds of schools across the country.

Student responsibilities (described on p 66) also offer rich opportunities for project and service learning.

Ref 18
p 112

Citizenship across the curriculum

In a citizenship school, the whole curriculum enhances young people's understanding of life, society and themselves, past, present and future. Learning is central to living a fuller, more enjoyable and varied life. Above all, learning gives people power over their own lives through greater understanding of themselves and the world, as argued in Chapter Three. Good topic work in primary schools creates connections between life and learning that form a foundation for understanding. At secondary level, many subjects can be enhanced and illuminated through their relevance to life. These connections can provide opportunities to develop an aspect of citizenship. Where and how these connections are made can be done by subject specialists using the grid on p 38. Older pupils could also do projects on citizenship and particular subjects, thus deepening their own understanding of both the subject and citizenship, which contributes to curriculum development.

Citizenship across the curriculum

Every subject can be used to develop skills and knowledge of citizenship and personal development, within the mainstream curriculum and through projects. All subjects include what can be termed 'powerful knowledge' – that is, ideas, information and skills that empower people to make a difference in the world. Understanding the nature of knowledge in the world is one of the most powerful gifts a teacher can give their pupils.

The following list suggests a few ideas.

Art
- illustrate or represent issues and topics from citizenship;
- look at representations of political and social ideas and movements in art;
- study origins and development of pigments, textiles and other materials used in art.

Design and technology
- impact of technology on culture and society;
- appropriate and sustainable technologies;
- design projects for the school and community.

English
- speaking, listening and oral skills are a prerequisite for effective citizenship;
- treatment of social and political themes in literature;
- origin of the English language as fusion of languages of conquered and conquerors;
- development of English through global expansion, colonialism and communication;
- varieties of English and literatures, within UK, Ireland, Africa, Asia and the Americas;
- use of language for persuasion and propaganda.

Geography
- relationship between economic and political decisions, landscape and place;
- impact of colonialism, trade, slavery, immigration and emigration on geography and demography, plant and animal varieties, national boundaries;
- role and effects of tourism and travel;
- climate change, environmental issues and sustainable development.

History
- development of economic and political ideas and institutions;
- influence of religious, political and economic ideas on events;
- impact of international events on national and local history;
- anniversaries and special events like Black History Month, UN Day, Armistice Day.

Home economics/food technology
- sources of food crops, spices and recipes;
- political economy of agriculture, food production, distribution and consumption;
- variety of cuisines and awareness of their cultural origins;
- health and nutrition in different cultures and continents;
- issues such as health and safety, nutrition, retailing, GM foods, biodiversity.

Modern languages
- the cultural and political contexts of each language;
- the origin of European languages in Sanskrit, Greek, Latin and other languages;
- the way in which words in different languages have different social meanings.

Mathematics
- use of number and maths to measure, calculate and understand the school, everyday activities and social issues;
- mathematics behind the headlines of political and economic events;
- use of maths to solve real world problems;
- use of number, maths and geometry in different cultures.

Music
- use of music for social and political purposes, to persuade, define status or promote ideas;
- musical projects in the community.

Religion
- diversity of religious traditions and value systems;
- development of a 'global ethic' and interfaith understanding.

Political understanding

Citizenship education includes 'knowledge and understanding of core concepts and conflicting political positions'.

Political understanding often develops through discussion and investigation of current issues as well as historical events. Time and resources have to be made available for this, not just through civic studies but across the curriculum. Citizenship schools encourage understanding of core concepts and current issues by:

■ Providing an appropriate range of local and national papers and magazines for pupils, parents and staff to read in an accessible place;

■ Creating time to discuss topical issues in circle or form time, or a specific lesson each week;

■ Organising mock elections alongside local, regional, national or European elections;

■ Inviting elected councillors, MPs, MSPs, MWAs and MEPs as well as members of other political parties to discuss specific issues with pupils or parents, and encouraging pupils to do research and role plays to prepare (see example at end of this list);

■ Taking part in model UN events;

■ Encouraging pupils to take up specific issues or causes they believe in and to set up branches of campaign groups through the school, on issues such as the environment (Friends of the Earth, Greenpeace, RSPB), human rights (Amnesty), housing (Shelter, Crisis), international development (Action Aid, Christian Aid, CAFOD, Oxfam, UNICEF, WDM), peace (CND, CAAT) or international co-operation (United Nations Association, One World Trust).

Young people need to be able to express the curiosity, doubts or commitment about social issues. Many pupils develop strong feelings about environmental issues, human rights, poverty, sexual orientation, religion, vegetarianism or school life. It is important that enthusiasm for a cause is not dampened, because human improvement comes from the passionate pursuit of particular convictions. But schools have a responsibility to enable pupils to develop their ideas and understanding by engaging with each other, other adults and the public debate on issues. The following example is one way in which this can take place.

Pupils speak with power

UNICEF provides useful free materials to help children from 8 to 18 'Put It To Your MP'. In 1999 over 300 schools took part, 250 MPs visited at least one school in their constituency, and 287 local newspaper articles featured MPs talking with children. Pupils raised topics such as smacking and violence; crime and punishment of young offenders; environment; immigration and asylum. At the most successful events, children engaged in real dialogue with their MP. As one 12-year old said, "I think this should be a regular event. I've never spoken to an MP before and it's a chance everyone should get to take." The materials include activities, information on the law and young people, draft letters to MPs and model press releases.

Ref 19
p 113

With all these issues teachers have a responsibility to ensure that pupils to 'recognise choices they can make, and the difference between right and wrong' (KS1), 'reflect on, express and explain viewpoints contrary to their own' (KS3) and critically evaluate such viewpoints (KS4), as set out in the national curriculum. Where particular political traditions are not strongly represented among pupils, teachers have a responsibility for ensuring that they get a hearing, either by inviting representatives of those positions into school, or by representing them themselves.

Through television, pupils are often aware of political issues from an early age and their ability to grasp fundamental principles is often underestimated. But the picture of politics in the media is often negative, giving a highly distorted view of the issues and political processes. Schools therefore have a responsibility to give pupils an insight into the backstage world of politics, by meeting politicians, observing Council meetings, visiting parliament, taking part in model parliaments, discussing issues in depth and campaigning on issues they feel strongly about.

Teaching controversial issues

Controversial issues are an essential part of the curriculum. They provide intellectual excitement and challenges, stimulating discussion, thought and the search for evidence. This deepens general knowledge, understanding and skills. They are also part of life. Young people will hear about them and have a right to learn about them and develop their own views. Moreover, some of these issues are crucial for their own future. Their views and decisions on them could have a direct influence on their own lives, so they need the skills and information to make up their own minds.

The 1996 Education Act aims to ensure that teachers present more than one side of controversial issues. Section 406 requires governing bodies and head teachers to forbid the promotion of partisan views in any subject and to forbid partisan political activities by pupils under 12 while in school. Section 407 requires pupils to be offered a balanced presentation or opposing views of political or controversial activities.

Teachers also have to be sensitive to the community served by the school, where some groups may have strong opinions on certain issues. Parents or pressure groups may be worried about bias or even indoctrination. These fears are rare, and it is even rarer for them to surface, but when they do, they can be vicious and damage the school, whether founded or not. This danger can be avoided through open and close relationships with parents and the community, so that the slightest concerns come to the school rather than fester. A clear policy on dealing with controversial issues, supported by the head and governors, is essential.

The Crick Report[39] contains a good discussion of these issues, on which the following points are drawn. All three main approaches to teaching controversial issues have both strengths and weaknesses:
a) The 'neutral chair' facilitates discussion without expressing any personal views while ensuring that a wide variety of evidence is considered and opinions of all kinds are expressed. However, this can be unconvincing and can even reinforce prejudices if pupils only hear what they want to hear.
b) In the 'balanced' approach, all aspects of an issue are presented as persuasively as possible, with the teacher acting as 'devils advocate' if necessary. This runs the risk that pupils see all sides as equally persuasive and do not develop the skills and information to counteract them. How issues are balanced is also critical: in a discussion of racism, racists and anti-racists would not be given equal

weight, but what about abortion, direct action, the drugs trade or pornography?
c) The 'stated commitment' approach means that the teacher starts by expressing their own views to encourage discussion. This has the advantage of being frank but is in most danger of accusations of bias and indoctrination.

These issues are by their nature controversial and do not have easy answers. In a democracy young people must be able to discuss them in depth. The guiding principle is that teachers should ensure that every issue is examined fairly and thoroughly, using a checklist of questions:
1. What are the main features of this issue?
2. Why is it an issue and who are the main protagonists?
3. What are their main interests and values?
4. What case do they make, what arguments do they use and how do they make them?
5. What to they say needs to be done and why?
6. What are the actual and possible consequences of their positions?
7. Who or what else might be affected by this issue, who may not have a public position or profile?
8. What evidence do different sides present, how can it be checked, and what additional information or opinions could be obtained?
9. What evidence would decisively refute or support a particular case, if any?
10. How, where and by whom are these matters dealt with?
11. How have they been dealt with in other countries or times?
12. How might this issue affect you and how can you express your point of view and influence the outcome?

Pupils should be able to say what issues they want to discuss and should have opportunities to explore difficult issues freely and in depth. Pupils can raise issues from an early age and form strong and sophisticated views which should be taken seriously. Controversial issues can arise in all subjects and can either be dealt with as they arise or referred to a special lesson, discussion club or other time. Drama, art, projects, debates and other methods can be used to explore issues in depth.

Enriching the curriculum
Overcrowded as the curriculum seems, we live in an information-rich society in which one of the key skills is being able to shift through large quantities of information to see patterns

and select what is important. These skills can be developed through many of the methods developed in this chapter. In addition, young people need opportunities to apply these methods to a wide range of subjects and topics not explicitly part of the national curriculum but very important life skills and knowledge for the modern world. These include:

■ education for sustainable development;
■ consumer education;
■ financial literacy.

These, can also be taught through special programmes, school conferences, short courses, activity weeks, off-site visits and residential field trips. Outside speakers and specialist agencies can provide a valuable input and greater variety of learning experiences. The world is so complex and diverse that teachers cannot provide the range of skills and knowledge needed to understand it, so other agencies and professions have to play their part in educating the next generation.

Student involvement in assessment

Sharing responsibility for learning means taking young people into one's confidence and actively involving them the process of reflection, repetition and feedback necessary for learning. In a democratic classroom, techniques for starting each lesson with pupils recalling key points from the previous lesson and recapping the main points at the end of the lesson can be lead by a pupil. In primary school, the class can round off the day with circle time for pupils to say what they have learned during the day and how they felt about it, as well as confirming any activities or messages for home.

Responsibility can also be shared by asking pupils at the start of a topic or course what outcomes they want at the end and what criteria they want to be assessed against, and how they would like to be assessed. This is usually easier in arts subjects, but in factual subjects some students like frequent short quizzes or texts, while in practical subjects a project or task may be more appropriate. Pupils are encouraged to take ownership of the outcome of their learning and how it is measured. If this process starts early enough, and is developed through increasingly sophisticated methods as children grow older, then pupils will gain in maturity as

well as responsibility. Records of Achievement Profiles are a powerful way of giving students greater control over recording and reflecting on their own progress.

At the end of each topic, course or term, pupils can be asked to write a self-assessment, backed up by evidence. Judgements must refer to specific pieces of work done during the term. Many pupils will be much franker and harder on themselves than a teacher. From about Year 3 pupils can be quite cynical about teachers' reports to parents, particularly those which are mainly positive, so involving pupils in writing their own reports can help everyone develop a greater honesty about attainment.

It is essential for teachers to be honest about the criteria and standards expected in the world. This means highlighting the importance of exam success for many career choices, but also acknowledging that exams are, by their nature, a system of discrimination and that some people succeed by studying later, or by following their passion to create an unconventional career. But there is no doubt that good grades at school make life easier later. However, where tests are frequent and treated almost as a game, many children will take them in their stride. Paradoxically, if young people treat exams as a choice, as a way of making life easier, rather than something they are forced to do, they will often be less anxious and do better in them. But for some children, exams may be an inappropriate way of valuing their talents and may even devalue them.

Assessment has to be treated first and foremost as a service for the learner, which provides an externally recognised benchmark and feedback, as well as tangible goals to work for. As an entry qualification for further study, training or employment, assessment should be appropriate to the skills and knowledge actually required. If assessment becomes an end in itself, there is a danger that it violates the fundamental freedoms of citizenship.

All standardised assessment is by its nature a system of discrimination. It judges people against a stereotype, a template or norm decided by the assessor. A 'reading age' is an average, a norm, that by definition will not apply to all children. Academic exams are based on a particular kind of intelligence, valued for a particular purpose, which may not be appropriate for ten, twenty or even fifty per cent of the population. Exams judge people by what they should be, rather than what they could be. When grades become identity, linked with status, and people are publicly classified by their exam results, there is a danger that they violate Articles 1 and 26 of the Universal Declaration of Human Rights.

Accreditation for achievement in specific skills, from driving and computer programming to languages and nursing, is a useful aid to learning. Accreditation is also a handy currency for employment. But it can never be the be-all and end-all of education, particularly when the world is changing so rapidly that many of the skills needed in the coming century may not even have come into existence yet.

A citizenship school will enable students to do as well as they can in appropriate exams, and also understand the role which accreditation and assessment play in society so that their development is not limited by examinations.

Self-assessment and evaluation

Taking greater control over the evaluation and assessment of learning is a powerful aid to learning as well as responsible citizenship.

If pupils feel trusted to make judgements about their work, and learn how to separate the judgement of their performance from their judgement of themselves, they develop self-confidence and skills in learning to learn.

Critical factors for self-assessment to develop effectively are:
■ a relationship of trust between teacher and pupils;
■ the ability of pupils to set (or negotiate) their own objectives and criteria;
■ the value given to pupil's own assessment of themselves; and
■ fun: the activity is enjoyable.

Self-assessment can take many forms. National Record of Achievement can be used to build self-assessment throughout a pupil's school career, starting in the nursery. If used sensitively as a basis for regular individual discussions with pupils (and parents in the early years) about their learning it can become a powerful aid to self-awareness and development. In some primary schools, teachers end the day by asking children to say what they have learnt and to anticipate what is coming next. In many primary and secondary schools, pupils contribute a self-assessment to the annual report to parents.

Activities for self-assessment and evaluation

● Instant scoring: at the end of an activity, lesson or course individuals are asked to rate their performance in one or more areas from 0 to 5. The areas to be rated can be suggested by the teacher or pupils and written on the board. For example: To what extent did I take part in the lesson? To what extent did I concentrate? How much did I enjoy the lesson/activity/course? The numbers are then collected in and a volunteer or the teacher calculates the average. The average and range can be presented then or at the start of the next lesson or activity. This provides instant feedback to pupils and teacher. It tends to encourage everyone to improve.

● Smiley faces: (this is a version of instant scoring for younger children) Draw three faces on separate sheets of paper (smile, straight mouth and frown), put them in three corners of the room and ask children to go to the face that best represents their response to questions about their performance.

● Wall meter: put squared paper on the wall so that pupils can create a bar graph of their responses to the questions such as those suggested in the first activity, as they leave the room.

● Evaluation wheel: ask the group to suggest criteria for evaluating their performance in a course or subject, preferably at the start, and come to an agreement about the main criteria (preferably not to many). Each criteria then becomes a spoke on a wheel, with zero at the centre and ten at the edge. Pupils then assess themselves on each of the criteria by marking a spot on the spoke.

● Computer-aided self-assessment, as developed by the Prince's Trust Study Support Programme.

Self-assessment can also be developed into peer assessment and pupil evaluation of lessons. (See p 88)

Part 2: Taking part: creating a learning democracy

> **Children have the rights to freedom of association and peaceful assembly.**
>
> *Article 15, UN Convention on the Rights of the Child*

Democratic schooling

Democratic decision-making is fundamental to citizenship. Citizenship schools give pupils, and other members of the school community, sustained experiences of decision-making to develop skills of participation and action. This means that every lesson and activity respects pupils' views, shares responsibility, promotes active involvement and encourages reflection.

A UNICEF survey suggests that between a quarter and half of all schools have democratic practices, although less than ten per cent have policies or lessons on citizenship education.[40] About half of secondary and a quarter of primary schools have student councils, but numbers are rising.

> *2. To develop skills of participation and responsible action, pupils should be taught to:*
> *a) use their imagination to consider other people's experiences and be able to think about, express and explain views that are not their own at Key Stage 4 critically evaluate such viewpoints;*
> *b) negotiate, decide and take part responsibly in both school and community-based activities;*
> *c) reflect on the process of participating.*
> **The Citizenship Curriculum, Attainment Target 3**

Shared decision-making requires appropriate structures to reflect the diversity of age, experience and roles within the school community. Rather than adopting traditional models of representative democracy, schools need to learn from them to create new models of participation capable of including all sections of the school community. These models include paired work, learning teams, circle time and representative councils for pupils, class meetings for parents, collegiate management by teachers and community associations involving the wider public. There are no blueprints, but plenty of experience to draw on.

Pupil participation

Pupils can participate in decisions in many different ways, starting with decisions over their own learning and conduct of the classroom as outlined in the previous chapter. This section looks at structures and processes to encourage wider participation, but there is inevitably some overlap.

Effective participation takes confidence, which can be fostered by a confidant. As a social unit, a classroom of 20 to 30 people is a lot to cope with, particularly when you are young. Structures for participation should therefore start with smaller units, such as pairs and groups of pupils, building up to classroom meetings and forums for the whole-school:

- learning partners and co-listening;
- a learning team or set, a group of five or six students;
- whole class circle time, meeting daily or weekly to develop relationships and resolve problems;
- classroom councils;
- a student council with elected representatives from each class and a meaningful role in all decision-making;
- school meeting or assembly;
- pupil representatives on the governing body.

As society becomes more complex and fluid, people play many different roles, with differing status, in many different groups throughout their lives. Citizenship schools offer many opportunities for people to develop confidence and skills in a variety of roles in different groups, but these opportunities need to be planned and supported. Otherwise the more confident pupils will always take the lead, while the less confident lose heart.

The ability to take part requires a foundation of self-confidence and self-esteem. The hurly-burly of school often erodes children's confidence. Many hide their vulnerability by teasing, bullying, swotting, playing the clown, sports or other roles. Roles provide an identity in which to hide as well as express oneself, a social niche in which to succeed at something. Even the dunce, joker and victim enjoy success of sorts. But many roles have a high price in terms of self-esteem and prevent pupils from taking part fully.

Schools contain many formal and informal groupings, from sports teams, lunchtime clubs and special friends to playground gangs. Often these are exclusive, involving only certain pupils. Teachers usually keep an eye on informal groupings and try to help a lonely child make friends or to break up gangs. A citizenship school aims to create a supportive structure for communication and participation that enables all pupils to take part, reducing the need for exclusive groups or gangs.

Learning partners

One-to-one support is the surest way of developing self-confidence. 'Learning partners' is a buddy system for pupils. It involves pairing pupils up when they start school, or even before, so that everyone knows at least one other person. Learning partners are not usually existing friends, because the aim is to build new relationships, although they usually become friends.

At its simplest, creating learning partners means asking one pupil to look out for another. But they can be used to set up mutual support for every member of the class. This means spending time as a class to talk through the role of a learning partner and reviewing it once a term.

Learning partners can be used to:
■ provide mutual support and encouragement;
■ share feelings (see co-listening below);
■ talk through key concepts or homework, to make sure everyone understands;

■ do joint projects;
■ share responsibility.

Many children form friendships which perform these roles, but these skills cannot be taken for granted. A growing number of children need help in making and sustaining relationships. For them, learning partnerships can create a subtle but lasting transformation in self-confidence, relationships and the ability to take part.

Co-listening (also called shared talk, paired listening or one-to-one time)

The ability to listen and to form a close relationship with another person are fundamental to personal development and democratic citizenship. 'Co-listening' is a simple but powerful process for pupils to develop listening skills, mutual support and a deeper understanding of what they are learning.

At its simplest, co-listening means pupils sitting in pairs, facing each other. Pupil A speaks uninterrupted about what they are feeling or anything on their mind for three to five minutes, while B listens. B then repeats what they heard A say. The pupils then reverse roles.

This exercise can be done at the start and end of each day. It gives every pupil individual, private, personal attention. At the start of the day it can help pupils express any worries they have and to say what they are looking forward to. At the end of the day it can be used to reflect on what has been learned during the day, or to share feelings about what has happened.

To introduce co-listening, it has to be demonstrated, either by the teacher with another adult or pupil, or by older pupils who have done it before. For the first year, co-listening can be part of the time-table, with supervised time set aside for it. Co-listening partners can be changed every week, fortnight or month, so that everyone pairs up with a variety of partners during the year. Where pupils are under emotional stress, it may be better to stay with the same partner for a term or more.

Pupils can be encouraged to continue co-listening throughout their time at school, by starting each term with co-listening exercises. As it becomes more familiar, pupils could be encouraged to chose a new partner at the

Taking part: creating a learning democracy

Creating a group identity

Most groups work better if they have a sense of identity, an agreed aim, clear ground rules and a sense of affinity as a group. This exercise can be used with learning teams, a whole class or other groupings.

Ask each group to:
- choose a **name**: suggest that each group brainstorms a list, then votes for one name;
- devise a **logo** and catch phrase;
- agree team **aims** and **ground rules**;

- create a group **collage or drawing** to show the interests and aspirations of the team.

These tasks can be introduced one by one or as a set, depending on pupils' age and ability. The exercise finishes with each team presenting themselves to the whole class. This can be done in a variety of ways including the use of display, a song, poem or drama if they wish. The name, logo, aims and rules should then be used throughout the year.

---

start of each week or half term, but make their own arrangements for co-listening outside class time. Even then, it is worth having a discussion about how it is going near the start and end of each term.

The learning team (or set)

Some pupils always get lost in a class of 20-30. A learning set or team is a way of building mutual support into a class so that no one gets left out. Learning teams are made up of five or six pupils with different needs and interests. To ensure diversity, they are not self-selecting. For example, one team might consist of three boys, three girls, one achiever, one non-achiever, and one child with special needs. It is easier to form permanent teams at the start of the year. Some teachers ask pupils to name five others they would like in their teams and include at least one of the five in their team.

Team members can be asked to take on a variety of roles, such as team rep (representative), scribe (who keeps a team log book), chaser-up (who makes sure commitments are kept) and chair (who leads team meetings). Roles can be rotated every half term, so that everyone takes a turn at having responsibility.

The primary role of the team is usually mutual support for learning. This can be enhanced by seating pupils in teams, by giving group tasks to the team, and by giving out results of tests and homework as a team, so that the class sees team results before each child gets their own individual results. Teams can also take on joint responsibilities within the school (see p 88) and be used for circle time (see below).

Circle time

I like circle time because we can discuss our problems and learn from our mistakes.
Primary Pupil

Circle time is a powerful and widely used way of developing empathy, relationships and values as well as resolving problems. Widely used in primary schools, circle time is increasingly being used by secondary schools, staff and even parents.

The central concept of circle time is very simple - everyone is equal in a circle and can share feelings, thoughts and experiences in a non-judgemental way to ensure that everyone is heard. In practice, circle time can become a rich and sophisticated process which transforms the school community. It is the heart of Jenny Mosley's whole school model for self-esteem and success through supportive and positive relationships, which shares many elements of a citizenship school. A range of resources that explain the model are listed in part 3.

Like any powerful tool, circle time can be abused, so it is important to be aware of the ground rules and structures which release its potential for personal and organisational development. Like any powerful technique, it also requires training and practice to use effectively.

The important elements of circle time for a citizenship school, are that it:
- is built into the timetable, either 15-20 minutes a day or once a week for 30-45 minutes;
- is an established forum for children to share feelings and thoughts, build trust, help each other and solve shared problems;

- follows clear rules created by pupils themselves;
- is supported by the school ethos;
- links into other systems, eg pupils can take issues from class to a student council;
- has a well defined structure, pace and aims.

While individual class teachers or form tutors can always do circle time with their own pupils, regardless of what other teachers are doing, it is best to develop a whole-school approach. For small schools, this means all staff (including midday and classroom assistants) training together. For a large secondary school, it may be best to phase in circle time, starting with Year 7.

> *It is essential that at primary school 'circle' teaching or interactive and experiential teaching is practised for both PSE and citizenship objectives*
> **Professor Bernard Crick, Chair, Advisory Group on Citizenship**

Ref 20 p 113

Classroom councils

A classroom council is a natural development of circle time, creating a structure for pupils to take on real responsibilities and develop citizenship skills. Classroom councils can be developed organically from circle time, starting with pupils taking turns to lead a circle discussion, and classroom council meetings can start with a circle time 'round' to share feelings and ideas.

The main difference from circle time is that a classroom council is a decision-making meeting of the whole class. Each class elects its own chairperson, vice-chair, secretary and, if the class has a budget, treasurer. Time needs to be built into the week for pupils to talk about their concerns. The agenda can be drawn up at the start of each meeting by going round the class in a circle, giving every child an opportunity to contribute. If there are more items to be discussed than there is time available, the class has to decide priorities or make more time later. All this requires skill from the chair and class members, which can be developed through practice and careful coaching by the teacher, another adult or an older pupil.

Classroom councils can deal with a wide range of issues, including behaviour, class rules, pupil responsibilities, problem solving, school improvement or community projects.

In the process, children develop self-confidence and skills in presenting arguments, listening to different points of view, working as a team and participating in formal decision-making. Classroom councils provide an ideal foundation for a whole school student council.

> *School councils and class councils ... can be a most excellent training ground in responsibility for future citizens; also an obvious sign that a school takes citizenship learning seriously!*
> **Professor Bernard Crick, Chair, Advisory Group on Citizenship**

Student councils

Pupil councils (often called school or student councils) exist in all kinds of school, from Infants to Sixth Form Colleges. They offer rich opportunities to learn about citizenship in practice, teaching skills, knowledge and procedures of representative democracy. For schools, student councils enable children to sort out their own relationships, improve behaviour, develop confidence and confront problems facing the school. They can support the authority of the school, strengthening the sense of belonging and consent among students, even if at times it challenges the authority of teachers or governors over particular issues. However, tokenistic student councils can be counter-productive. If pupils can only discuss minor issues decided by teachers and cannot have any influence on school life, the council soon loses credibility and increases cynicism.

Ref 21 p 114

> *Children and adults together are able to rebuild the culture in which they live.*
> **Professor Robert Moore, Foreword, Pupil Councils, 1993**

There are several different models of school councils, depending on the size, nature and philosophy of the school. See Resources (from page 103) for more detailed guides to setting up and running a student council. School Councils UK provides a wide range of advice, material and training.

The main features of a Student Council are:
- a council of pupil representatives, usually two from each class;
- a link teacher to support the council (who can be the head);
- a code of conduct or rules for meetings;

School councils: Secondary

Lipson Community College in Plymouth has about 1,200 students. It uses circle time in class and has elected councils for each form. The agenda of each meeting covers successes, current issues, new issues and environment. The councils have helped to reduce vandalism, brighten up public areas, redesign the school uniform, improved attainment and behaviour, and improved food. The feeder primary schools also have schools councils.

Cotham School in Bristol is an 11-18 school with 1,200 pupils and a 100-member student council representing each tutor group. The council is chaired by two sixth-formers and meets every five weeks, in lesson time, attended by the head teacher. Two pupil representatives from the council attend governing body meetings, where they can speak but not vote, and have to withdraw when confidential matters are discussed. Councillors also sit on five action teams, dealing with catering, charity work, environment, equal opportunities and facilities. Each team is supported by a teacher and a parent volunteer, providing organisational and secretarial support. The council had a role in awarding the school's catering contract, for which students visited another school to see the caterer in action. The equal rights action team organised a display about where pupils come from to raise awareness about diversity. Alex Parsons, a 16-year old pupil said, "I've seen our council develop from a disorganised rabble to a body that can debate issues affecting us in an organised and serious way – I'm proud to have been involved in that." The council has strong support from the head teacher, James Wetz, who points out that academic results have also risen since the council was set up."

■ a constitution, setting out aims, powers, membership, election procedures, conduct of meetings, officers, executive and sub-committees, finances and other matters;
■ a budget, so that students can afford to carry out decisions; and
■ training for student councillors and executive committee members.

The optimum size is about 20-25 pupils attending, which means 40-50 councillors if about half do not attend the meeting. Primary councils usually elect two pupils from each class. Larger schools often split into two or even four councils, either for

Years 7-10 and 11-13, or vertical splits into 'Houses' consisting of representatives one or two classes from each year.

'It was clear from the schools we visited which had such councils that rules and behaviour were among the issues regularly discussed. We consider that the main advantages of schools councils is that pupils are able to discuss school policies openly and make positive suggestions. This encourages a sense of collective responsibility.
Our impression is that where they exist, pupils are likely to make responsible use of them. We would however discourage the creation of token councils.'
The Elton Report, Discipline in Schools, 1989

The success of a Student Council depends on active support from staff and students, followed by its size, powers and training for student councillors. Students need to feel that the effort they put in will make a difference, otherwise they will lose interest. This means that:
■ decisions are implemented wherever possible;
■ the council has its own budget;
■ there are formal channels of communication between the council and staff, and if possible governors as well; and
■ there is frequent and effective communication with pupils, through form time and assembly as well as newsletters.

Council elections, meetings and decisions should be treated as important events for the school, with proper nominations procedures, election campaigns and ballots. Councillors should receive some training, ideally through peer education by retiring councillors. Notes should be kept of meetings, and they should have a meaningful role in all decision-making.

It may not be possible for all decisions by a student council to be carried out, but they should be taken seriously. If proposals appear impossible, it is worth exploring with pupils their reasons for the proposal, since there may be other ways of achieving their goals, and to give a considered response why the staff or governors consider them to be impossible. Pupils should be able to present their proposals to a higher decision-making body, such as the governors. Learning citizenship in practice includes dealing with authority, disappointment and defeat. But if pupils are really determined, they should be able to improve and pursue their case through the school.

School councils: Primary/Middle

Middle School

Wensum Middle School in Norwich created a school council to give pupils a say in how the school could improve. In the past, pupil's opinions were canvassed through class discussions, questionnaires and small group interviews, but the school wanted to give pupils a strong voice in school improvement. Through the council, pupils have been involved in reviewing the drugs policy, which led directly into schemes of work. The council also addresses issues brought up in classes and the suggestion box.

"Being a councillor is important because you are responsible for making the school a better place for everyone else. It is cool, because we've changed things. We've sorted out a litter rota, we've got new playground markings and games, and we've got a playtime buddy system. We are also getting more drinking fountains. We've made a big difference." Student councillor

Primary School

Rowlatts Hill Primary in Leicester has 300 pupils. The pupil council has introduced equipment and other improvements to the playground, decided on charities for which the school collects money and raised concerns about the curriculum.

Windsor County Primary in Toxteth, Liverpool, has weekly classroom council meetings and a school council. Pupils discuss school policy and take part in issues such as discipline, extracurricular activities and anti-bullying strategies. Councillors provide governors with a half-termly written report and send occasional letters to parents. They organised a fundraising raffle by collecting items for a hamper. The money paid for each class to have a differently coloured games box for playtime. Class representatives took responsibility for looking after the equipment.

The head teacher reported "Teacher pupil relationships have improved, there are no incidents of vandalism or truancy. Disruptive behaviour has diminished. ... The school council received favourable positive comments from OFSTED".[42]

Student assemblies (or school meeting)

A student assembly is a meeting where students themselves set all or part of the agenda and conduct the business. This can be an important experience for those running it, but boring for everyone else if done badly. However, with practice, students can become very confident and capable of addressing large groups. It can be a very special event, at which students present issues and ideas arising from the student council. At St Christopher's School, Letchworth, The Schools' Council is made up of Year Group Representatives, who report back to the whole school meeting where decisions are discussed and ratified, or amended.

Pupil representatives on governing bodies

Growing numbers of secondary schools have student representatives on the governing body. Although children under 18 cannot legally be members of the governing body, they take part as observers and their views are taken into account.

The extent to which pupil participation on governing bodies is meaningful depends on how much information and support they get before and during meetings, and how seriously their views are taken. Given that governing body meetings are often long and boring, and that adult members can feel excluded, the careful introduction of meaningful pupil participation can lead to improvements all round.

Appointment of staff

Student involvement in appointments is an essential element of a citizenship school. It develops teamwork, judgement, a sense of belonging and a shared responsibility for the school community.

A growing number of schools involve children in choosing new teachers. At Hampstead School and Technical College students have been involved in selecting teaching staff for several years. All applicants have to teach a lesson, usually in Years 8 or 9, which is evaluated by pupils using a questionnaire. For the appointment of deputy head, the student council chose a panel of five students, who drew up their own questions based on their criteria for a

Challenges of pupil participation

Head teacher Bernard Trafford describes difficulties with staff over his attempts to introduce greater pupil democracy and the importance of being very clear about what it means and where decision-making power lies. On the whole, teachers and pupils valued the Student Council, greater openness, a sense of equality and sharing of information. Teachers felt that "It makes for security all round. Students can feel that if they have a serious grudge or problem they can say something. Also for staff. … Everyone feels valued, they work together and learn."

But several teachers were concerned about "the risk of loss of respect for those in authority." As one said, "an approachable headmaster cannot put the fear of God into awkward kids. They have to learn for themselves where to draw the line." When parents wanted students to attend parents' consultation meetings, this was opposed by a majority of staff. Teachers resented the head's attempts to raise the topic again, at parents' insistence, but a pilot scheme eventually lead to a change in policy for year 11 and above.

After six years the majority of teachers and students felt that the school had become more democratic and was a better school as a result. 'Added value' exam results also improved by 23% during the same period, and an inspection report noted the positive benefits of pupils feeling 'valued and empowered'.

Trafford concludes, "Sharing power within school takes courage. … Students and teachers have to learn new skills of negotiation and compromise. At times the difficulties can seem intractable. … Yet evidence of the value of participation is overwhelming. Teachers talk of their sense of being valued. Students … speak confidentially of what has been achieved and argue articulately for the further changes that are needed."[43]

Breul high school in Zeist, Netherlands, has involved pupils in teacher appointments for twenty years. A task group of 15-year old pupils meet weekly for training, including team-building and practice interviews. They are supported throughout by a teacher, who acts as a facilitator and co-ordinator, evaluating and giving feedback to the pupils. They read all application forms and select three teachers for interview. They write a report on each applicant for the head teacher, which is taken into account in the selection process. Pupils are fully aware of how important and sensitive this work is, and the need for confidentiality. The pupils' voice counted for a third of the final judgement in the teacher's appointment. The process is not considered threatening by new teachers. Pupils are then involved in appraising new teachers during their probationary year (see p 89).

At Highfield Junior, the Student Council was talking about the need for new staff and a boy asked, "Can we be involved? We need to know who is joining our team?" There is no rule to stop pupils from being involved in staff selection and now all appointments involve pupils.

Ian, a pupil, describes the process: "First we talk in circle time about the sort of questions we need to ask, and what sort of answers would be good for the school. Each class chooses the best person to ask their questions. Last time, there were two of us from each class, eight altogether and one teacher who didn't say anything. We each asked one question. … [Afterwards] We counted up the stars we gave them, and the one we thought would be best for the school got five."

The children did their interviews first. The governors' do their interview and decide, before reading out the children's decisions. In most cases they coincide, but when two applicants appeared equally strong, the governors were influenced by the children's decision to give more emphasis to music and sport.

A new class teacher said "The interview with the children was the best part of the day and it made me want to come and work here. The interview took about 15 to 20 minutes and they had obviously planned the order of questions carefully. For me, that was the interview."

good deputy head. In the interview, the children told the applicants something about the school and then took turns in asking one question each. The candidates were rated out of ten on each question, and then the school governors considered the children's recommendations.

Another secondary school invited applicants for deputy head to present an assembly which was evaluated by pupils as part of the selection process.

All candidates are advised of the children's role in selection and they have all been very positive. The aim is for the children to identify what qualities and talents each person can bring to the school. It is not about setting children up in judgement about adults.[46]

Pupil appraisal or evaluation

Pupils continuously evaluate teachers' performance, but they rarely have a role in staff development, appraisal, inspection or routine quality control. This is understandable, particularly since teachers' are under so much external pressure. But where learners and teachers are partners in a joint endeavour to increase human knowledge and welfare, pupil feedback should be standard practice, like applause at the end of a play, evaluation after inset or the everyday feedback that is part of all good teaching.

A few examples of pupil evaluation have already been mentioned - in the selection process of new teachers at Hampstead (p 86) and the feedback to newly qualified teachers at Sharnsbrook (p 72). Any teacher can ask at the end of every lesson what pupils liked most/least about the lesson, what they found easiest/hardest, and to rate the lesson out of 10. This short activity gives the teacher instant feedback, develops pupil's skills in evaluation and builds trust between teacher and pupils. Introducing pupil evaluation like this can be awkward at first, but once it becomes established it becomes second nature and can even be managed by a pupil as a student responsibility.

At de Breul high school, Zeist, Netherlands, new teachers have a probationary year before being appointed. Their lessons are evaluated twice during the year, in November and April, by the head of department, a manager and pupils from a range of classes taught by the teacher. Pupils complete an extensive, confidential questionnaire on teaching and classroom management (see p 89), which is given to the head teacher.

Taking part: creating a learning democracy

Democratic Education: Learning from Europe, VLIB Survey

Before you begin, read the instructions
• Fill in this opinion survey carefully and on your own
• The result of this survey will influence the future career of your teacher
• Don't forget to put the name of your teacher
• Only tick one answer (yes/no/no opinion)
• If you have ticked the wrong square, please tick the right square and put a circle around it.

	Yes	No	No Opinion
A			
1. Does the teacher explain clearly the contents of the lesson?	☐	☐	☐
2. Is the structure of the lesson clear at the start?	☐	☐	☐
3. Do you know beforehand what to expect from the lesson?	☐	☐	☐
4. Does the teacher respond adequately to your questions?	☐	☐	☐
5. Does the teacher regularly review your homework during classes?	☐	☐	☐
6. Do you learn to conduct your own study during classes?	☐	☐	☐
B			
1. Does the teacher indicate clearly what subject-matters will be included in tests?	☐	☐	☐
2. Does your teacher make clear what (s)he expects in your answers on test questions?	☐	☐	☐
3. Is your teacher consistent in her/his requirements towards all students equally? (e.g. homework, tests)	☐	☐	☐
4. Do you think that your teacher marks your work fairly?	☐	☐	☐
5. Does your teacher return your work within a reasonable time?	☐	☐	☐
C			
1. If the class has problems with a method of teaching, does your teacher address and discuss the problems voiced?	☐	☐	☐
2. Do you get on with your teacher?	☐	☐	☐
3. Do the class and your teacher get along with each other?	☐	☐	☐
4. Has your teacher set out clear behavioural rules during class?	☐	☐	☐
5. Does your teacher apply rules concerning latecomers, talking and eating in class consistently?	☐	☐	☐
D			
1. Does your teacher conform to the school requirements concerning arriving late, smoking, drinking in class?	☐	☐	☐
2. Does your teacher conform to the school rules concerning tests?	☐	☐	☐
3. Does your teacher conform to the school rules concerning homework-free weekends?	☐	☐	☐
E			
1. Does your teacher make the lessons interesting?	☐	☐	☐
2. Is your teacher enthusiastic about her/his subject?	☐	☐	☐
F			
1. Are your teacher's classes orderly and under control?	☐	☐	☐

G
1. Any additional comments/and or observations should be set out in the space below.

Student participation in and beyond school

In many areas students already take part in forums beyond the school. Cambridge has run young citizen's juries. Islington's Get Smart, Take Part promotes youth participation. Some local authorities run youth councils. In Birmingham, primary school pupils support the Lord Mayor's charities, learn how the City Council works and debate real issues in the Council chamber as part of the 'First Citizen' scheme. The Young People's City Council is a ward-based assembly of up to 150 Youth Councillors aged 11-14, elected through schools, which meet every half term. Birmingham is also creating a dedicated auditorium for young people's events, Millennium Point, with video conferencing facilities to involve people throughout the world.

Aylesbury Vale Youth Council has 24 members, elected or nominated by schools, colleges and youth organisations. The structure shadows the district council and has a similar committee structure, with direct links to council departments. It has campaigned on traffic calming and concessionary bus fares, organised events and run a grants programme for the district and county council.

In Manchester schools and youth organisations have elected 100 representatives from 12 to 18 years old to sit on the city's Young People's Council. Election turnouts are said to be 80-90%. Youth councillors demand action on issues from homelessness, transport and play facilities to bullying. They proposed peer-counselling to deal with bullying, and obtained a budget of £18,000 to set it up.

Kirklees IYCE Initiative (Involving Young People Equally) was set up in 1997 to change public services from within, underpinned by the Kirklees Children's Plan 'Young Citizens' charter. A consultation on making routes to school safe used 'graffiti walls', peer video interviews, questionnaires, suggestion slips and prioritising photographs to make an input into planning by the Highways service, but came up with useful recommendations for other services as well.

Many European countries have national federations of pupil councils or pupils' unions. In Sweden the pupils' union has individual members, aged 14-18, and the federation of pupil councils, SVEA, has representatives from a third of all secondary schools and facilitates dialogue among pupil councils and with policy makers. Holland has an active National Pupils Action Committee (LAKS), which promotes youth participation. It prepared legislation on pupils' councils in schools which was ratified by Parliament. In Denmark the government routinely consults the pupils' union. In Germany, there are often pupils' councils (or 'conferences') at district, regional and national levels, funded by the government, with cross representation which includes teachers, parents and other interests on consultative bodies for education.

At a European level, the Organising Bureau of European School Student Unions (OBESSU), founded in 1975, has representatives from 22 European countries, which co-ordinates and runs events, provides information and develops joint policies. In 1995 it adopted a European School Student Rights Charter.

Ref 22 p 114

Children's (or youth) parliaments

Britain held its first Children's Parliament in 1998, when sixty 11 year olds quizzed cabinet ministers and presented their White Paper to the Prime Minister at the Palace of Westminster. The next stage was to present their proposals to the European Parliament. More than 100,000 children from 3,500 schools took part, through debates and essay competitions in nine regions.

There are local and national youth councils in many European countries, involving young people in local life through dialogue and projects. A recent study showed that these councils gave young people from different social and cultural backgrounds a sense of social usefulness. In France, the national assembly debates and usually approves a piece of legislation proposed by the youth assembly. Youth Planet is an European association of children and youth councils which organises European-wide meetings of young people.

Ref 22 p 114

Taking part in global decision-making

To change the plight of the disadvantaged, to overturn the burden of third world debt, requires an appreciation of political process, an understanding of global economics and a hard-headed

realism about how change is achieved, and not solely a well-meaning upsurge of social and human conscience. That is why the ... the development of the curriculum to provide a politically literate nation, is so important to us all.
David Blunkett, MP, Secretary of State for Education, 5 June 1998

Young people's lives are increasingly affected by global events. The worldwide web makes it possible for anyone to communicate instantaneously with people in every country, although access to the web is still relatively limited and dominated by Europe and North America. So much of our culture, economy and society is inextricably linked with the rest of the world that lack of international awareness is a serious disadvantage. We all need to see ourselves as citizens of the world as well as Europe, the United Kingdom and a nation.

Citizenship schools aim to give pupils experience of international issues through direct involvement as well as development education and activities such as model UN General Assemblies (MUNGAs), security councils or other international bodies. These events give young people opportunities to simulate international meetings by representing different countries and arguing over real issues.

Pupils should be taught about
i) the world as a global community, and the political, economic, environmental and social implications of this, and the role of the European Union, the Commonwealth and the United Nations. (Key Stage 3)
j) the wider issues and challenges of global interdependence and responsibility, including sustainable development and Local Agenda 21. (Key Stage 4)

Young people today can directly influence global decisions. At the World Summit for Children at the UN in New York in 1990 a child volunteer was assigned to each of the 71 world leaders and played a significant role. At other UN events children have held preparatory events and elected a representative to read a prepared statement to the delegates at the main event. Young people's voices have often increased the sense of urgency among global decision-makers.

Most development agencies, such as Action Aid, Christian Aid, Oxfam, Peacechild International and UNICEF, produce high quality materials to support education on international issues.

Ref 23
p 115

Parents' participation

Citizenship schools aim to involve all parents in their children's learning as well as the governance of the school. Parents are the first and often biggest influence on children's attitudes to school. Many of today's parents did not have a positive experience of school. Until the mid-1980s, when most of today's parents had left school, three out of four 16-year olds achieved less than five O-level passes or equivalent. School taught them that they were failures. Just over a third continued in full-time education. For many of today's young parents school was also disrupted by battles between teachers and government over pay and conditions. Since then levels of attainment have risen, so that now over half of all 16 year olds gain the equivalent of five O-levels and over 70 per cent continue in full-time education. Schools still need to overcome negative experiences among parents.

As well as negative experiences of school, many parents from all backgrounds find parenting itself very demanding. Uncertainty and instability are now normal for many families. Parents feel under pressure and insecure in their roles, often with less support from their own parents and the community than in the past. Over 70 per cent of mothers and a quarter of fathers suffer depression in pregnancy. Relationships between partners often become strained after the birth of a child. Domestic violence, child abuse and emotional neglect may affect one in ten young people.[45] Mental illness among children is rising, affecting one in five, and an increasing number of children 'are unpracticed in making and consolidating friendships, dealing with conflict, the taking of risks and team games'.[46] One in seven adults suffer mental disorder at some time, often tracing the origins to childhood. These statistics emphasise the importance of emotional and intellectual development at home, and the fundamental role of families as places of learning.

Parents' active involvement in their children's learning from birth is essential for raising achievement. Until all children and parents experience schools as a rewarding pleasure, rather than a duty to which they must submit, it will be hard for schools to generate the joy of learning and the practice of citizenship.

School improvement is building on sand without serious and sustained support for families as the foundation of learning. Every school, local authority and the government have a major interest in ensuring that parents are supported and take an active part in learning. These arguments have been developed elsewhere,[47] but it is worth emphasising that parents are first among equals in the education of their children, not consumers of education services, but citizens of a democratic society who pay for schools through their taxes.

Schools have many different ways of working with parents, but the following four formal structures can strengthen parents role as 'learning citizens' of the school.

These structures are:
■ class meetings (or associations) of all parents of children in each class;
■ parents' councils consisting of elected representatives from each class;
■ parents' representatives on the governing body, as at present;
■ parents' representatives on a whole school council, if it exists.

For most parents, their child's class is the main point of contact and concern. Research shows that there is no consistent link between pupils' achievement and parents' involvement with the school through parent-teacher associations, participation in extra-curricular activities or visits to school. Parental involvement makes most difference to pupils' achievement when it 1) provides structure, that is, reliable routines at home and co-operation with school when problems arise, and 2) active involvement in the child's learning at home - constructive monitoring and guiding the child's use of time, explaining concepts, reviewing homework, supporting the child through difficulties. School can help parents in this role through class meetings, which also create a two-way channel of communication between parents and the school.

Ref 9
p 108

Ref 24
p 117

Class meetings

A class meeting (or association) consists of all parents of children in each class, meeting two or three times a year to discuss the curriculum, concerns about the class and issues affecting the school, as well as to socialise and support the class. They are widespread on the continent and being developed by a growing number of schools in this country, such as Rush Common Junior in Abingdon, Oxfordshire.

Many schools hold class meetings for parents and pupils when they first join the school or for specific purposes, such as before a school trip or subject options. These meetings are usually concerned with information giving and an option for parents or pupils to ask questions. Some schools, however, have built on these meetings to create a lively forum for all parents to become actively involved in school life.

The main advantage of class meetings for parents is that they offer a regular opportunity to meet with other parents and teachers directly involved with their own child. They can be an enjoyable social occasion as well as a source of information and mutual support. They can also give parents direct influence in the class and school.

Class meetings are used to:
■ get an overview of the curriculum;
■ address issues/concerns;
■ discuss school policies and changes;
■ enable parents to get to know each other;
■ organise social events;
■ elect class representatives to the Parents' Council.

The format of class meetings varies according to how well established it is. When they start they are usually run by teachers, or sometimes a teacher and parent together, but more established meetings are run by an elected chair or group of parents. Established meetings can have 'contact groups' of six to ten parents, who agree to share information with each other if they are unable to attend meetings.

Meetings take many forms. Sometimes parents sit in a circle, sometimes in groups of six to eight round tables, cabaret style. Most meetings include time for the teacher to talk about what is being covered in class, sometimes with a more detailed presentation on a particular subject, a discussion of parents' concerns, and a social element. The best meetings have a sense of occasion about them - music playing when parents arrive, light refreshments, then a brief presentation followed by discussion. As a result, parents get much more involved in the class, making things, fund-raising and organising outings, arts or sports activities, or other events.

The class meeting offers a political forum for parents. Although most discussion is about everyday education and life at school, the meeting provides an opportunity for parents to discuss issues they feel strongly about. Usually this will be about the school, but it may concern the local environment, transport to school or other issues affecting the community.

Parents' councils

Class meetings provide a natural basis for Parents' Councils (or associations), which usually consist of two elected representatives from each class, one father and one mother. Larger schools may have a Year Council, with two parent representatives from each class or form, and then a number of representatives from each year for the whole school.

Parents' groups and initiatives

Sometimes groups of parents feel that the school does not adequately address their needs, or they want to organise additional activities. A citizenship school would respond constructively and encourage parents' initiatives.

Many schools already have parent-run supplementary schools, groups for black or Muslim parents, parent action groups on the environment and other interests. A few schools even make facilities available to parents educating their children at home, or allow their children to join specialist lessons such as languages, information technology or sports. These are all part of the process through which schools are becoming centres of lifelong learning.

But parents' initiatives can raise considerable challenges. Not all are necessarily positive, so it is important to have a fair and effective procedure. To give a few examples: A group of fathers want to organise sports activities, but they have a very fixed idea about who they want to involve and how, raising concerns about racism and sexism. A group of ethnic minority parents want to set up supplementary classes, teaching their own faith, history or language, but a group of white parents mobilises in opposition. A group of parents want to organise a community festival in the school, but there are concerns about lack of experience, costs and safety. A faith group wants to run after-school classes for children, but use harsh discipline, including verbal abuse and physical punishment.

All parents' initiatives are opportunities to develop citizenship in practice, increasing skills and experience for everyone involved. In almost all cases, it is important to welcome the positive intent in the initiative and then negotiate to ensure that activities are broadly consistent with the school's agreed values. Someone in the school, usually a staff member, has to take responsibility for building relationships with the group. If there are difficulties, they need to be identified as early as possible and dealt with openly. It is particularly important to work out the aims of the group and what is needed to achieve them, so that the group and school can agree who will do what.

> *Schools do not understand our children's needs and do not spend enough time talking to us parents.*
> *I needed to solve this problem of our children's religious needs in school.*
> *I joined the Parent Consultation Group and now we interview parents, teachers and children about what they would like in their schools.*
>
> **Refugee Somali woman,**
> **Bristol Community Education**

Both the school and parents need to discuss potential difficulties in an open and constructive way, without personalising issues. In many cases, the group may be able to change, or the school can be flexible over particular points. But it is essential to be firm about fundamental values concerning racial discrimination, sexism, safety and treatment of children. If the group cannot meet certain requirements, it may mean that they cannot work with the school, but it is important to remember that the issue will probably remain in the school community and needs to be addressed, or it may grow into a grievance which is harder to deal with.

Finally, agree an action plan, stating who will do what when. At this stage it may be appropriate to involve other agencies, to help overcome difficulties and support the initiative. It is important that both sides keep to their agreements in any action plan.

This process is itself a piece of citizenship education for both the parents and the school. When parents and community groups set up all sorts of different groups round the school, it enriches the life of the school and the community.

The governing body

Parents' representation on the governing body is the one official, formal presence of parents in decision-making. Many schools actively encourage parents to stand for election to the governing body. A contested election to the governing body generates awareness as well as discussion of issues facing the school. During the year schools can promote their governing body through a noticeboard displaying photographs of all the governors, together with copies of the agenda, minutes and other information, as well as a governor's newsletter or column in the school newsletter. Links between governors and the school can be strengthened by making each governor responsible for liaison with an individual class or year, or with a subject area.

The visible presence of the governing body as the main policy-making body for the school shows citizenship and representative politics in action. The issues are real, although not party political, and the decisions have a direct influence on school life.

Whole school council or community association

Where school premises have several different users, such as a youth club, health service or library and community groups as well as the school itself, it is worth having a regular meeting of representatives from all user groups to discuss issues affecting the whole school community.

Parents' forums

Some education authorities, like Enfield in London, have a termly meeting for parent representatives from every school in the borough. In Enfield the meeting is often attended by the Chief Education Officer as well as officers responsible for specific topics to be discussed. The agenda usually has one item chosen by the parents and one chosen by the LEA, and any matters arising from previous meetings. All schools are represented by parents, usually a parent governor, although some head teachers also attend.

Parent representation in local and national politics

Since June 2000, every local education authority has to have an elected parent governor representative on the education committee. It would be a relatively small step for these representatives to form a national Parents' Council, as advocated by CASE, the Campaign for State Education.

Ref 14
p 117

Most European countries have national parents' organisations, many of them strong and well-funded, and either national parents' councils or representative bodies on which parents are represented. Parents are consulted on all education reforms as a matter of course.

Staff participation

The teaching profession can no longer be so easily ignored or be treated by powerful elites as a necessary group who are part of someone else's design.
David Hargreaves, The Challenge for the Comprehensive School, 1982[48]

High staff morale and sense of personal power are essential for schools to develop citizenship. If teaching or support staff feel powerless, they will stop pupils, parents or other members of the school community from exercising power. Staff who fear empowered pupils or parents will blunt budding citizenship, leading to frustration or conflict. At the same time, staff themselves need to be a real part of the decision-making process, in which their views are valued and make a difference. A sense of power among staff is therefore vital for citizenship schools.

But the role of staff is complex, and it is important that a citizenship school recognises this. All school staff are in many ways like civil servants. They are there to provide a service for pupils, parents and the community, who govern through the governing body and elected politicians who allocate funds for the school. Yet because they are permanent, professionally trained and salaried, staff exercise considerable power over what happens. Like the civil service, power is organised through a hierarchical line-management structure. Officially most power and responsibility is vested in the head teacher, although in practice this varies widely.

Teaching staff are traditionally the most powerful members of a school community, with authority over pupils and parents. In practice, however, many teachers feel that their authority is flouted, their work is constrained by an unrelenting timetable, an inflexible curriculum, unruly pupils, hostile parents and a ruthless inspectorate, and they have little power or resources to do anything. Although they have much more power than any pupil or parent, it may not feel that way.

It is vital that all staff are also citizens of the school, not just servants. There are many different ways in which this can happen, but four essential requirements are:

- support for the personal well-being and power of each staff member;
- a collegiate style and democratic ethos;
- effective formal representation at all levels of decision-making;
- the school is a learning organisation, in which all staff are continuously learning and the school responds creatively to changing circumstances.

Formal representation does not necessarily mean that the school is either democratic or a proper citizenship school, as illustrated by the following example.

Staff well-being and power

I see all the teaching and support staff as an upright circle of dominoes. If any of those dominoes is in a bad mood or negative state of mind, it has the power to knock down all the others.
Jenny Mosley, Quality Circle Time

Staff participation which does not acknowledge the importance of personal power and morale can lead to paralysis or a culture of opposition, as described above. Citizenship is a creative, constructive process, not a formality.

Jenny Mosley's Whole School Model for Quality Circle Time is a practical approach to developing self-esteem which starts with the teacher's well-being. Relationships in the classroom start from our relationship with ourselves.

A collegiate style of leadership

British education puts a great deal of emphasis on the leadership role of the head teacher as a chief executive, but other successful education systems have a flatter structure and more collegiate style. The word 'college'

Challenges of staff democracy

A large city comprehensive school adopted a democratic decision-making structure, in which all policies had to be approved by a meeting of all staff (teaching and ancillary), at which a representative number of students also had a vote. Proposals had to come up through various constituencies (departments, pastoral teams, unions, students' council, parents' association, management meeting, etc) via the Agenda Sub-Committee, which was chaired by a member of the Senior Management Team (usually the head). Proposals would be circulated in advance, then had a first reading discussion and were voted on at the next meeting, to allow all constituency groups to discuss it.

While this structure appeared to be both logical and democratic, it often polarised opinion, reduced effective participation and paralysed change. Decisions that were approved might have a 60:40 majority, but divided staff into winners and losers rather than create shared ownership. Proposals were diluted to win majority support. Management proposals were frequently defeated and a pattern of collective opposition developed among staff, who used their majority to prevent change. "Oppositional manoeuvrings between and within the staff became more important than improving the practice of teaching and learning." [49]

Many schools which experimented with formal structures for staff participation will recognise this description. As teachers become tied up in working parties and meetings, decision-making becomes paralysed and sometimes even the main purpose of the school becomes lost. The answer is not to abandon the attempt to democratise education, but to recognise that the school is a complex community in which many different forms of participation are needed.

has the same origins as colleague, meaning 'chosen together' from the Latin *com-* (with) and *legere* (to pick). Many schools in German-speaking countries, as well as Steiner schools in Britain, are run by a college of teachers who choose one of their number to act as a chair or head for a year or so. In many Spanish schools, teachers elect a head to serve a term of four years, although pressures of the post in urban areas mean that candidates can be hard to find.

Transforming nightmares: what's the worst that could happen?

This exercise aims to help staff express their fears and explore responses to them. It is best used when planning to introduce a specific proposal, such as circle time, class meetings for parents or student councils. It can be used with staff on their own or with teachers, parents and governors.

Participants sit in groups of about 5-7, round tables or in a circle. Each group has a flip chart. Groups can be mixed (teachers, support staff, parents and governors together) or separate (teachers with teachers, etc).

With every group, each person takes turns to complete the sentence

'The worst thing that could happen is ...'

One person lists key words on flip chart paper.

All groups share their lists and then each group chooses one or two of the 'worst case' scenarios to prepare a

positive response that would turn the situation round, including any training needed to ensure that everyone is capable of taking part.

Each group then presents their strategy to the whole group. These can be written up, refined and used for action planning if desired.

For this exercise it is important that the facilitator or senior staff have already considered some of the worst things that could happen and can show how it could be dealt with successfully.

It is essential to finish the exercise on a positive note: Each table does a sentence completion with: 'The best thing that could happen is ...'

Each table then draws up a list of the benefits of the innovation and finally each individual says what they personally will do to make it a success.

Leadership is a complex set of qualities and skills, and an important function in any organisation. Different times and circumstances require different leadership styles, and schools may suffer from inappropriate, as much as poor, leadership. The cooperation of colleagues and members of the school community is as important as the leaders' abilities, and successful schools have many leaders with clear responsibility for aspects of school life.

A citizenship school encourages all members of the school community to develop leadership abilities, by taking responsibility and sharing decisions. It is able to choose appropriate leaders for different tasks and circumstances, and does not dump all responsibility on the head or a few individuals.

Staff representation

The example on page 95 highlights the difficulties that can arise from a purely formal structure of staff participation. At the same time, the absence of formal representation for groups of staff can also lead to divisions and dissatisfaction, particularly between teaching and support staff, part- and full-time, or in large schools.

Inclusion of representatives of support staff and part-timers in staff meetings, working

parties and key committees can help to ensure real participation and involvement by all sections of the school staff.

In large schools, problems due to size can in part be overcome through 'Houses' or 'mini-schools' with a relatively high degree of autonomy within an agreed policy framework. To prevent Houses from becoming too inward-looking, staff member could rotate between Houses every five to seven years.

Whole school assemblies or meetings

School assemblies have considerable potential to become forums for citizenship. They give pupils, staff and parents opportunities to develop skills and confidence to address large groups. They can also be used for formal stages in the democratic process concerning the annual report, school development plan, changes to the school constitution or even elections. School assembly can address serious issues or even crises facing the school, but more often they are occasions for developing its vision and values through song, stories and shared experiences, or for celebrating achievements. But for pupils or parents to be able to participate effectively in large groups like an assembly, they need lots of experience of speaking in front of smaller meetings.

Community participation

Citizenship schools blur the dividing line between school and community. Growing numbers of schools are already becoming community centres, offering other adult education, arts, sports and leisure on site, or even developing into a 'full service' school, with library, health centre, leisure facilities and other facilities. Like many Cambridgeshire schools, Arthur Mellows Village College, Peterborough, is used seven days a week. The Governors Community Sub-Committee includes representatives of the education authority, school staff, adult education, user groups, local primary schools, the police and other agencies.

In School Inclusion, Mog Ball[50] shows how schools are working with other agencies and families to create what a full service community school with 'wrap around' provision for children, including early mornings, after school study support and holiday activities. In Scotland the government is already piloting full-service community schools.

Where school premises are used by other agencies or if it has close relationships with community groups and services active in the local area, citizenship schools have a **community association** or **council** to run shared facilities and activities.

Community ownership

Citizenship schools could ultimately be owned and run by the community they serve. Real ownership could give communities a strong incentive to maintain, improve and develop the use of their school as a centre of the community. Local management of schools gave schools greater control over their own affairs. In most cases it enabled schools to manage resources better, meet local needs more easily and innovate. Community ownership would take this one step further, enabling schools to have stronger relationships with local people, as is often the case with church or community schools.

Some communities already feel they own their local school, but legally it belongs to the local authority or the church. Local people may have paid for the premises through taxes, improved them through fund-raising over generations, or even set it up in the first place through the parish, but they do not really own the school. Local or national government can change its character, transfer assets or even close it down. Hundreds of communities have lost playing fields, buildings or schools as a result of decisions beyond their control. Although the authorities may have good reasons in their own terms, losing facilities or a whole school can have a deeply damaging impact on a local community.

Closing or changing the character of a school involves stringent procedures, but the process often teaches people that they are powerless as citizens. They can protest, but they are subjects petitioning the ruling power rather than citizens deciding for their own community. Occasionally people save a school from closure, which can stimulate greater involvement, but they rarely gain real control over the school. Some form of legal ownership and control is therefore a crucial test of democratic schooling.

There are times when a local authority feels it needs to change the way it allocates money for school places. This is inevitable. Difficult decisions will always arise. The issue is how local communities are involved in such decisions.

In practice, this means that certain legal and financial rights should be vested in the local community, such as:

- legal ownership, in the form of a community trust or charter;
- community rights to use the facilities by all ages for learning and community cohesion;
- rights to raise finance through bonds or other prescribed means, as a not-for-profit agency;
- rights for the whole community to have a say in major changes.

Control over finance is a crucial test for community ownership, local democracy and public participation. Radical thinking is also needed if all parents are to have real power over local provision and address inequalities within each area. To increase the potential of schools as significant social units, people need real ownership and control over their local community school. Local management of schools and devolution of responsibility to governing bodies has already produced a significant shift in power from the days when most spending decisions were made at the town hall. There are still teething problems as school governors and staff learn new skills, local authorities and the government attempt to establish fair funding formulae, and education support services become more customer orientated, but devolved powers will not be removed. If anything, there needs to be further devolution of powers to parents at a class level. Many schools also want more responsibility for maintenance and even capital spending.

Participation in running local schools has considerable potential as the first step towards greater local democracy and a more pluralistic system of public services. New forms of community ownership could give local people direct control over individual schools, with powers to raise loans for capital spending, improve premises and transform provision in response to local needs. There will still be a role for elected local or regional government to take strategic decisions over the allocation of public funds. But most decisions over the management and content of education could be made by families and their all-purpose local community education centre.

Holland and Denmark both have a system of education funding which enables groups of parents to get state funding for schools. As a result both countries have a greater variety of schools following many different curriculum models. In Britain, the Third Sector Alliance[51] is campaigning for a similar approach to diversity within the state system.[52] This issue is inevitably clouded by our class-based private school system, which is educationally and socially divisive. Greater variety and community control within the state system could erode the economic base of privileged private education by creating better alternatives at a local level.

In some United States school districts, local communities have this kind of control over their school, where a referendum is used to decide on raising bonds to invest in school facilities. School boards campaign for public agreement to borrow money or raise local taxes through local referenda, so that major education spending decisions involve the whole community.

Part 2: **Building a new learning constitution: the role of government**

> **All human beings are born free and equal in dignity and rights. They are endowed with reason and conscience and should act towards one another in a spirit of brotherhood.**
>
> *Article 1, Universal Declaration of Human Rights*

Sustaining learning citizens

The pace of change today requires a learning revolution in which schools have to involve all members of the school community as 'learning citizens'. Rapid developments in knowledge and technology mean that young people may be just as likely to introduce new ideas, information, skills or equipment to adults as the other way round. Teachers can no longer be the gatekeepers or sources of knowledge, but facilitators of learning. All members of the school community - pupils, parents, staff and local communities – need to develop greater control over their own learning and share responsibility for the school as a community. But teachers and schools have an increasingly important role in enabling young people to develop the attitudes, skills and values needed to take part in the complex, global knowledge economy evolving around them.

A citizenship school is one in which all members of the school take part as free citizens. Every aspect of school life encourages participation, shared ownership and responsibility. This means creating many different forms of participation, appropriate to the particular pupils, place and context of each school.

School is an important focus for two crucial periods of most people's lives - as children growing up, then as parents. Many schools also play a larger role in the community, as a centre for under-fives, adult education, leisure and community events. It is a place to meet, a source of community, contacts and information, and often a resource centre as well. Schools are increasingly involved in fostering learning in families, offering access to the internet and providing a local gateway to further learning opportunities for adults.

Schools have more potential to develop a deeper sense of community and social cohesion than is possible through almost any other institution, particularly for young people and parents. Schools provide a framework for a wide range of agencies to work with young people and families, both in and out of school hours. As society fragments into a bewildering choice of goods, television channels and interest groups, the ability of schools to a create a focal point for many different local communities becomes increasingly important.

As community learning centres, citizenship schools can also offer the experience of democratic participation and a sense of power over one's own life, as a learner and member of society. Politics need not be a remote and often unreal activity that dominates the news, but part of everyday decision-making over behaviour, the curriculum, resources and activities in school and society, stretching from the classroom to global issues.

The new national curriculum for personal development and citizenship offers schools the opportunity to renew and transform themselves from the bottom up. This transformation could be even more important for our society than the extension of democracy through votes for all or universal education, because it could give every individual greater power over their own lives and the ability to take part in a complex institution such as a school. With this insight and experience, people would learn how to shape other institutions that affect their lives. In the long term, the creation of citizenship schools could deepen democracy more than any other constitutional reform.

How the local education authority can help

Local education authorities can do a create deal to encourage, support and develop citizenship schools by:
■ affirming and supporting good practice;
■ helping schools to share experience, ideas and information;
■ co-ordinating policy development and joint projects;
■ organising training;
■ providing a resource centre of materials, information and contacts;
■ developing guidelines and policies;
■ creating learning neighbourhoods, towns and cities;
■ modelling good practice; and
■ providing access to council departments, statutory services and political processes.

A single local authority adviser or officer can make a big difference by the way in which she or he works with schools, by either practicing citizenship or by stifling it. Ideally, the whole authority would develop a commitment to citizenship schools, leading from the front with a commitment in principle from elected members, providing advice and support along the lines outlined here. Citizenship schools would form a key part of policies for lifelong learning, learning towns or cities, social inclusion and economic regeneration.

In every LEA there are schools with some elements of a citizenship school outlined in this book. A few schools may even be doing most of them. Simply identifying and affirming existing good practice is an important first step to promoting citizenship schools. Current practitioners have the potential to become champions for specific elements of citizenship schools. It may be worth involving teachers, parents or older pupils in an 'appreciative inquiry' (see p 71) to find and learn from current practice. Such an exercise could contribute to an accredited qualification for some participants, such as the OU Certificate or an OCN credit.

The next step is to create opportunities for schools to share experience, ideas and information about what they are doing, through twilight sessions or a conference for schools to celebrate their work and involve pupils in elements of citizenship schools. The opportunity to present a piece of work or project to a wider audience, through a performance, exhibition, the press or television, can be an experience of a lifetime. One underused way of sharing experiences is for teachers to visit other schools and if possible take part in activities.

The third step is to create a steering group or network to develop and promote citizenship schools across the authority. This should start by bringing people with a shared vision to develop a broad strategy. But to become effective, the group will need to involve powerful allies and even potential opponents - to apply citizenship skills in building support and neutralising potential opposition.

These steps will identify both strengths and gaps in the development of citizenships schools. Good practice can be disseminated by involving teachers and other school members in training and joint projects for other schools. Depending on the LEA, it is sometimes best to start by getting a policy commitment from elected members and then promoting it among schools. In other LEAs it is best to build awareness and support among schools before bringing proposals to elected members.

Either way, it is worth building up a resource centre of materials, information and contacts for schools to use. In a large authority, resources could be made available through schools in different areas, so that schools themselves become part of a citizenship resource network. In addition, it is worth developing a website, an email contact list and newsletter, to share information.

LEA guidelines and policies can help schools produce their own policies. It is not neces-

Building a new learning constitution: the role of government

sary for LEAs and schools to reinvent policies on citizenship education, but the process of drawing up a specific policy is an important part of citizenship in practice.

Joint projects are another way of strengthening partnerships for citizenship. Projects might include training and support for initiatives such as peer meditation, quality circle time, Learning through Landscapes, Changemakers, student councils, etc; or joint events, such as a model UN, a town youth council, Put it To Your MP, etc; or the shared development of citizenship schools across the authority.

The creation of a learning neighbourhood, town and city can help to mobilise businesses, community groups, public services, libraries, museums and other facilities to create an integrated network of provision and support for lifelong learning. This can give schools additional support and places to take children for learning in the community.

A powerful way for the LEA to support citizenship is to model good practice by involving schools and the local community in an open, accessible and accountable way. Many of the elements of citizenship schools can also be applied to the LEA. Above all, it can seek to work in a co-ordinated coherent way, according to consistent values which empower staff involved in service delivery. The LEA can develop policies in partnership with schools and support parents' forums, youth councils and community schools to involve people effectively, as many LEAs do already.

As part of local government, LEA advisers and officers can also improve access to other council departments, statutory services and political processes. Local forums for Agenda 21, council tenants, planning, transport, single regeneration budgets and other issues can all increase opportunities for pupils and local people to influence decisions affecting their lives. But community participation and consultation has become discredited in some areas because councillors and officers pay little attention to the outcomes and people have no influence over the allocation of resources or what happens on the ground. Citizenship has to be meaningful, and when it is, people will make a positive contribution to improving their area.

Finally, local government staff can use national associations of local authorities, advisors and other professional interests to share experience and promote support for citizenship schools.

Ref 25
p 116

How central government can help

For central government, citizenship schools are a way of involving all members of a school community in school improvement and community development as well as implementing the citizenship curriculum. Citizenship schools have the potential to support a wide range of national policies for social inclusion, economic development and lifelong learning, as summarised on page 6.

However, the purpose of citizenship schools is not to implement government policies, but to empower members of the school community as citizens of an increasingly democratic society. This means that schools may choose to pursue policies different from those of the government. In a mature and diverse democracy, this will enrich society, as it does in Holland and Denmark, where there is much greater diversity within state education. As society changes, schools will be able to respond in different ways, generating a greater variety of approaches to education, from which the whole country can learn.

The government can do a great deal to promote citizenship schools:
■ promote the concept of citizenship schools as a model of school self-improvement;
■ provide funds for training and development of school citizenship;
■ a national network and resource centre to support the development of citizenship schools;
■ offer grants for independent projects which support citizenship in schools, such as peer mediation, service learning, thinking skills, student councils, circle time and other elements outlined in this book;
■ support a national system of recognition or accreditation for citizenship schools, with the prospect of additional funding and freedom, provided certain conditions are sustained;
■ encourage closer relationships between schools and their communities by providing funding for community education use of school premises all year round;
■ create a national youth parliament and

encourage the formation of local youth councils;

■ support national organisations of school students and of parents to strengthen their voice in national policy-making;

■ create a representative national schools forum or commission of parents, young people, teachers and others with an interest in school education to develop and scrutinise education policy proposals;

■ continue to develop the national curriculum as guidelines rather than prescription.

These measures could unleash greater creativity and commitment to learning in schools and their communities. They would encourage schools to make the citizenship curriculum come alive in the everyday life, and give schools a wider role in their local community. Above all, they would enable schools themselves to develop the capacity to respond to the relentless pace of change in knowledge, society and the economy.

In the longer term, citizenship schools should be recognised as a special category of school, which have earned the right to take control of their own curriculum as a result of a process involving all the elements set out in this book. It may be that citizenship schools should also have achieved a certain level of attainment among pupils and have put in place a framework of quality assurance and self-evaluation which ensures that self-determination does not become self-delusion on the part of a powerful minority within the school. Given these safeguards, the government should recognise the potential of self-governing citizenship schools as the best guarantee of Britain's economic prosperity, social cohesion and rising standards of educational attainment.

What I like best about my school

This simple exercise aims is an approach to school improvement that starts by getting people to look at what they think the school does well in order to build on these things (see appreciative inquiry, p 71 for details). It can be used with pupils, staff, parents or the community. It can be used as part of any process of consultation or planning, or as part of an induction programme or school leaving exercise. It may be particularly useful when the school is going through a hard time, such as after a negative Ofsted report or criticism in the press.

In essence, it involves people asking a few key questions, which can be refined to focus on a specific aspect of the school.

1) **What do you like best about school [or an aspect of school]: be as specific as possible? OR: What do you think the school does best [in general or about the specific aspect being investigated]?**

2) **What could be done to make this even better?**

3) **When you first came to this school, what was your dream [OR: what did you hope for]?**

4) **If you could improve one thing about this school [or aspect], what would it be?**

This exercise is best done by young people, asking adults or other young people. It is important for people asking the questions to practice first, to be comfortable about them, and to overcome any cynicism, so that they are asked in a way that people want to answer honestly and thoughtfully.

It can be a useful part of data-gathering for work on the school development plan or a specific aspect, such as policy on behaviour, special needs, the environment, etc. Questions always need to be refined to meet the specific situation. Who is asked will depend on the focus, but it is particularly useful to ask a wide variety of people who are in a position to see what is going on in the school, such as the school secretary, caretaker, mid-day assistants, nurse or others who visit the school on a regular basis for particular tasks.

These questions can also be given to every pupil before they leave the school.

The benefits of this exercises are that it 1) focuses on the positive; 2) shows people that the school is interested in their views; 3) is about school improvement; 4) helps to identify areas for improvement; 5) helps to motivate people to bring about improvements; 6) involves pupils. Asking these questions, particularly number 3, can also help to re-kindle hopes and visions for the school.

Results from such a survey can be collated into a report or an exhibition for the whole school to see.

Part 3: **Resources**

The following sections describe a small selection of the huge amount of books, materials, organisations and other resources available to support citizenship schools, organised in order of chapters in Part Two. The inclusion of materials or trainers does not constitute a recommendation, since schools' needs differ and organisations change. Resources have been included to provide practical advice, information and insights from a wide variety of sources to encourage schools to learn from the wealth of knowledge and experience available today. Where possible, addresses and websites are given to make access easier.

A book or video can be very helpful in developing new ideas, but they are usually not enough by themselves. It is important to plan, prepare and, if possible, train before introducing any technique or method such as peer meditation, circletime, student councils or class meetings for parents. Then regularly review how things are going. Activities can become cosmetic and routine if not refreshed.

Most of the following resources have been tried and tested within the school system, but schools can learn a great deal from the arts, business community development and other sectors. Businesses spend more on education and training than the government, and get better people and performance as a result. The arts can convey important ideas faster and more powerfully than classroom teaching. Community involvement can create motivation to learn a wide range of skills and abilities.

Citizenship schools are willing to learn from the whole world, using and adapting anything that enhances learning for all. These first few books give unusual insights into citizenship, democracy and participation in different contexts.

Freedom to Learn, by Carl Rogers, 1983, ISBN 0 673 20012 1. Explores the personal abilities needed to teach in ways that people can become free and effective. Examples and stories from schools in the United States.

Maverick!, by Ricardo Semler, Arrow Books, 1994, ISBN 0 0932941 7. A remarkable story, warts and all, of how an engineering company became more successful by becoming more democratic. Workers make most decisions, recruit and evaluate their own managers, and have access to the company books. Reads like a novel, buzzing with ideas and insights about the process of transformation in a tough environment.

The Learning Revolution, by Gordon Dryden and Jeannette Vos, 1994, ISBN 0 905553 43 8. Using recent research into the brain, outlines the challenges and opportunities for learning.

The Living Company: Growth, learning and longevity in business, by Arie de Geus, 1997, ISBN 1 85788 185 0. Written for business managers, this is a description of 'learning organisations' by its originator and an important discussion of the shift to a knowledge society. Not strong on democracy but full of insights about the importance of play, learning and values for organisations.

Chapter 4: **Creating a culture of citizenship**

1. **Changing the school constitution**

Changing our School by Highfield Junior School. The story of how one school transformed itself, in the words of pupils, teachers and other members of the school community. Available from Loxley Enterprises Ltd, PO Box 55, West Park, Plymouth PL6 7YQ tel: 01752 513858 email: publox@aol.com

Change Forces: Probing the Depths of Education Reform, by Michael Fullan, Falmer Press, 1993, ISBN 1 85000 826 4. A study of the difficulties and challenges of educational change at a school and social level, full of insights and practical ideas. "Managing moral purpose and change agency is at the heart of productive educational change."

How to improve your school, by Tim Brighouse and David Woods, Routledge, 1999, ISBN 0 415 19444 X. This is an inspiring, humane and practical guide to school improvement, full of ideas and insights for leadership in schools, for which "a consistent set of values is the first necessity".

The Empowered School: The management and practice of development planning, by David Hargreaves and David Hopkins, Cassell, 1991, ISBN 0 304 32293 8. A pragmatic guide to school development planning and school improvement, although it only mentions in passing that "Parents and pupils usually contribute fresh, positive ideas".

The Quality School, 1992, *The Quality School Teacher,* 1993, and *Control Theory in the Classroom,* 1986, by William Glasser, HarperCollins. Influential books on improving schools, consistent with the approach of citizenship schools. Glasser's three key concepts are 1) focus on quality, 2) eliminate coercion, 3) persuade students to evaluate their own work.

For values education see Ref 11

2. Creating fair rules and boundaries

21st Century Discipline: Teaching students responsibility and self-control, by Jane Bluestein, Scholastic, 1988, ISBN 0 7682 0049 0. Information from website: www.janebluestein.com

3. Conflict resolution and mediation

Materials
The Co-operative Classroom: a behaviour resource pack for primary schools by J Gilmore & P Dymond.
Available from LINKS Educational Publications, The Dingle, Pontesbury Hill, Pontesbury, Shropshire SY5 0YN tel: 01743 790 029

Creative Conflict Resolution: More than 200 activities for keeping peace in the classroom, by William J Kreidler, Scott Foresman & Co, USA, 1984. Mainly for nursery to Year 7. Available from Friends Bookshop tel: 020 7663 1030

Crucial Skills: an Anger Management and Problem Solving Teaching Programme for Secondary School Students by Penny Johnson and Tina Rae. Ten lessons and follow-up work to help students develop self-esteem and constructive strategies of dealing with anger. Available from Lucky Duck Publishing, 34 Wellington Park, Clifton, Bristol BS8 2UW tel: 0117 9732881

Let's Mediate by Hilary Stacey & Pat Robinson. A comprehensive guide to peer mediation for infant, junior and secondary schools. Available from Lucky Duck Publishing, 34 Wellington Park, Clifton, Bristol, BS8 2UW tel: 0117 9732881

Nonviolent Communication: A Language of Compassion, by Marshall B Rosenberg, Puddle Dancer Press.
website: www.puddledancer.com

Playing with fire: training for the creative use of conflict, by N Fine and F Macbeth, Youth Works Press, 1994. For young people over 12. Available from Youth Works Press tel: 020 7272 5630

Students Resolving Conflict: Peer Mediation in Schools, by Richard Cohen, GoodYear Books, HarperCollins, 1995. A comprehensive guide with step-by-step assistance for setting up a peer mediation group in secondary schools by the co-founder of School Peer Mediation Associates in the US. Available from Friends Bookshop tel: 020 7663 1030

Trainers
Catalyst Consultancy,
320-1, The Custard Factory, Digbeth, Birmingham
tel: 0121 442 1222

Jenny Mosley Consultancies, offers whole-school approach to behaviour and self-esteem. Jenny Mosley Consultancies, 8 Westbourne Rd, Trowbridge BA14 0AJ tel: 01225 767157 email: circletime@jennymosley.demon.co.uk website: www.jennymosley.demon.co.uk

Jessons Mediation Project,
Jessons CoE Primary, School Street, Dudley

Learning Foundation runs training in non-violent communication.
The Learning Foundation, Worting House,

Basingstoke, Hampshire RG23 8PY
tel: 01256 811887
email: learn@compuserve.com

Newham Conflict and Change,
2a Streatfield Ave, East Ham, London E6 2LA

Mediation UK, 82a Gloucester Rd, Bishopston, Bristol BS7 8BN tel: 01272 241234

Signal Point offers a pack of initiatives on youth facilitation, mediation and talking through trouble.
Signal Point, Station Rd, Swindon, Wilts
tel: 01793 514596.

Southwark Mediation Centre,
Cambridge House, 131 Camberwell Rd,
London SE5 0HF

Transforming Conflict offers training and consultancy in whole school policies to deal with conflict, build self-esteem, reduce bullying and exclusions. Belinda Hopkins,
Transforming Conflict, The Flat, Mortimer Hill, Berkshire RG7 3PW tel: 0118 933 1520
email: b@transforming.u-net.com

Turning the Tide, Quaker Peace and Service, Friends House, 173 Euston Rd, London
NW1 2BJ tel: 020 7388 1977
email: qps@gn.apc.org

4. Maintaining the physical environment

There is now a lot of support available for involving young people in improving the environment, from local community groups and councils to national agencies.

British Trust for Conservation Volunteers (BTCV) offer training, support and resources for volunteers in nature conservation and work with schools. They produce handbooks and *The Practical Conservation Pack, Advice for Teachers.*
BTCV, 36 St Mary's Street, Walingford, Oxfordshire OX10 0EU tel: 01491 821600
website: www.btcv.org

Changing Places: children's participation in environmental planning by Eileen Adams & Sue Ingham, The Children's Society, 1998, ISBN 1 899783 00 8. A wide-ranging book on how children of all ages can take part in changing the world around them. Includes twenty case studies of work in schools and the community, with practical advice for project planning, organisation and development.

Community Links have a national network of local contacts, including community safety officers. They produce an annual of innovative ideas, many by young people, on community safety, full of practical projects which can be applied in schools and communities. The two latest volumes are:
• *Ideas into Action:* community safety ideas aimed at and generated by young people
• Visible Voices: young people's ideas for community action
Community Links, 105 Barking Road,
London E16 4HQ tel: 020 7473 2270

English Nature produce materials for site managers and older students, some of which can be adapted for other age groups.
English Nature, Northminster House, Peterborough PE1 1UA tel: 01733 455000
email: enquires@english-nature.org.uk
website: www.english-nature.org.uk

Learning through Landscapes provide extensive materials and support for schools involving pupils and adults developing their grounds as the 'outdoor classroom', including *A Guide to the Management & Maintenance of School Grounds,* by Joan Wood and Michael Littlewood.
Learning through Landscapes, 3rd Floor, Southside Offices, The Law Courts, Winchester SO23 9DL tel: 01962 846258
website: www.ltl.org.uk

School Works is a secondary school design initiative by the Architecture Foundation. It involve pupils in improving school buildings to enhance educational achievement, pride and pleasure in schools. The Foundation invites schools to send ideas and join a School Works database.
School Works, The Architecture Foundation, 30 Bury St, London SW1Y 6AU
tel: 020 7839 9389
email: mail@architecturefoundation.org.uk
website: www.architecturefoundation.org.uk

Shell Better Britain Campaign encourages effective community-based sustainable development by providing project grants,

information and support for a network of 26,000 community groups sharing good practice and experience. Information Sheets cover a range of topics including Travel to school, Trees, Energy efficiency, Fundraising and Setting up a web site. Interactive, its newsletter, is a mine of information on issues, projects, funding and practical activities. Newsletter and information sheets available free from
Shell Better Britain Campaign,
King Edward House, 135a New Street,
Birmingham B2 4QJ tel: 0121 248 5900
email: info@sbb.co.uk
website: www.sbbc.co.uk

Sustrans Safe Routes to Schools is a National Lottery backed project to make walking and cycling safer with a strong emphasis on involving children, parents and teachers. Information on funding, a free newsletter full of case studies, and free materials with advice on a range of topics including safe cycling, walking, health and how to develop a School Travel Plan. Teachers' Resource Packs and Project Packs are available to buy.
Sustrans, PO Box 21, Bristol BS99 4HA
tel: 0117 929 0888
email: schools@sustrans.org.uk
website: www.sustrans.org.uk

Tidy Britain Group produce a wide range of materials and sponsor both The Greenfingers Challenge and Eco-schools. The Greenfingers Challenge is a horticultural competition with up to £1,500 in prize money for group projects (not just schools), with a useful Start-up Pack for participants. Eco-schools is a Europe-wide scheme involving 200 schools in the UK.
Materials from Tidy Britain Group include:
• *Environmental Education and Tomorrow's Citizen, A video and materials for in-service training,* by Robert Stephenson
• *Inside Out: an action plan for improving the primary school environment,* by Cherry Mares and Robert Stephenson
• *Look Around the Town: First Steps in Understanding the Urban Environment* (4-7 years)
• *Our Environment* (7-11 years), published by Nelson & Son
• *Beating Litter* (all ages: Teacher's Handbook)
Tidy Britain Group, FREEPOST, The Pier, Wigan WN3 4EX tel: 01942 824 620
The Greenfingers Freephone Hotline:
0800 783 7838

Woodcraft Folk have produced two useful packs for citizenship and the environment:
• *Let's Grasp the Nettle: an Environmental Education Pack for work with 9-13 year olds,* with games activities and projects for young people to explore issues which concern them.
• *Let's Take the World in Hand: an Environmental Education Pack for 13-16 year olds,* for 30 sessions with over 60 activities and projects for young people to explore their environment and take action to protect and improve it. Includes additional materials for residentials and special events.
Woodcraft Folk, 13 Ritherdon Rd, London SW17 8QE tel: 020 8672 6031
email: folk@woodcrft.demon.co.uk

5. Improving playtimes

"Can I stay in today Miss?" Improving the School Playground by Carol Ross & Amanda Ryan, Trentham Books, 1991, ISBN 0 948080 42 6. A practical guide to involving children in improving playgrounds and addressing issues like bullying, equal opportunities, environmental improvement, play. For primary schools; also relevant to secondaries. Trentham Books, 151 Etruria Road, Stoke-on-Trent ST1 5NS

Create Happier Lunchtimes, WEST and *Guidelines for Midday Supervisors,* Positive Press, both by Jenny Mosley. Available from, JMC, 8 Westbourne Road, Trowbridge BA14 0AJ tel: 01225 767157 email: circletime@jennymosley.demon.co.uk

Playtimes & Playgrounds–The Book! by Angela White & Jane Wilkinson, Lucky Duck Publishing, 1996, ISBN 1 873942 51 6. A guide to improving playtimes in primary schools, with a good guide to activities and further resources.
Lucky Duck Publishing, 34 Wellington Park, Clifton, Bristol BS8 2UW tel: 0117 9732881

6. Communications

APT, Association of Professional Theatre for Children and Young People. A voluntary organisation of 160 theatre groups who work with young people. Also runs *Take Off,* England's only annual theatre festival for children and young people.
APT c/o CTC (Cleveland Theatre Company), The Arts Centre, Vane Terrace, Darlington DL3 7AX tel: 01325 352 004
website: www.apt.org.uk

Children's Express is a news agency for young people aged 8-18, which places stories in the national press.
Children's Express, Exmouth House, Pine St, London EC1 tel: 020 7833 2577
website: www.childrens-express.org

ITC, Independent Theatre Council, is the umbrella organisation for small-scale touring companies including local theatre in education.
ITC, 12 The Leathermarket, Weston St, London SE1 3ER tel: 020 7403 1727
website: www.itc-arts.org

Making a Leap: Theatre of Empowerment, A practical handbook for creative drama work with young people, by Sara Clifford and Anna Herrmann, 1999. This book presents a flexible, holistic model for training young people in drama skills, including personal development, group work, conflict resolution and facilitation skills.
Available from Jessica Kingsley Publishers, 116 Pentonville Rd, London N1 9JB

National Association of Youth Theatre has links with 650 youth theatres across the country which run workshops and perform.
NAYT, Arts Centre, Vane Terrace, Darlington DL3 7AX tel: 01325 363330
email: naytuk@aol.com
website: www.nayt.org.uk

Theatre in Education is an international company that focuses on empowering young people to find solutions to issues such as bullying, drugs, racism, sexism and violence. Methods include forum theatre, psychodrama and theatre workshop.
Theatre in Education, Holloway School, Hildrop Road, London N7 0JG
tel: 020 7619 9115 email: tie@tietours.com
website: www.tietours.com

Theatr Fforwm Cymru uses 'forum theatre' to work on issues like friendship, relationships, gender, bullying, substance misuse and HIV/AIDS. Works with primary and secondary schools, as well as staff in education, health and social services. Theatr Fforwm, Goodwick Community Education Centre, New Hill, Goodwick, SA64 0DH tel: 01348 873805
email: fforwm@aol.com

Video in View, by Jim Mulligan and John Westwood, CSV, 1994. A set of materials on using video, based on the work of students at Mayfield High School. Available from CSV, 237 Pentonville Rd, London N1 9NJ tel: 0207 278 6601

Youth Cable Television, 77 Barlby Road, London W10 6AZ tel: 020 8964 4646

Chapter 5: **Learning freedom: the empowering classroom and curriculum**

7. Developing a sense of self

Most activities listed in Part 3 can help to develop a sense of self. Circle time (Ref 20) is primarily aimed at building self-esteem, but everyday achievement in class, purposeful activities and positive relationships are just as important for developing resilience and self-worth. There is a danger that over-emphasis on positive self-image and feeling good can undermine real self-esteem if children do not have opportunities to do well and make a tangible contribution.

The following are just a few of the many books and materials that can help parents and teachers develop children's self-worth:

All Round Success, by Jenny Mosley, West Publications, 1991. Written with teachers and full of practical ideas of how to enhance children's self-esteem. Available from
JMC, 8 Westbourne Road, Trowbridge BA14 0AJ tel: 01225 767157
email: circletime@jennymosley.demon.co.uk

An Early Childhood Curriculum: From Development Model to Application by Eva L Esa and Penelope Royce Rogers, Delmar Publishing, 1992. A detailed curriculum handbook for structured child-centred learning, full of practical exercises as well as theory and illustrations.

Confident Children; Self-Esteem and *Self-Motivation,* all by Gael Lindenfield. Published by Thorsons tel: 0870 900 2050
website: www.thorsons.com

National Pyramid Trust for Children is a charity that offers schools a system to identify and support children experiencing difficulties due

to low self-esteem and lack of confidence.
National Pyramid Trust for Children,
204 Church Rd, London W7 3BP
email: mailbox@nptrust.freeserve.co.uk

Positive Parenting: Raising children with self-esteem; Motivating your Child: tools and tactics; Self-esteem for Boys: 100 tips and *Self-esteem for Girls: 100 tips,* all by Elizabeth Hartley-Brewer.
Information from Vermilion,
Random House UK Ltd tel: 0207 840 8400
email: enquiries@randomhouse.co.uk
website: www.randomhouse.co.uk

Smallwood Publishing for materials on self-esteem for schools and parents.
Smallwood Publishing, Chartlont House,
Dour St, Dover, Kent CT16 1ED
tel: 01304 226900

The Place to Be offers a programme of emotional and therapeutic support to children in schools through trained staff and volunteers. Supported by the DfEE.
The Place to Be, Edinburgh House,
154-182 Kennington Lane, London SE11 4EZ
tel: 020 7820 6487
email: p2b@compuserve.com

See also Ref 12, Emotional Literacy

8. Developing a sense of purpose

The following books for adults contain insights, exercises and information that can be used to develop a sense of purpose in learning and bring depth to careers education.

Richard Bolles's work has become an essential resource for American career guides. Full of stimulating ideas, information, activities and eccentric illustrations. *The Three Boxes of Life,* Ten Speed Press, 1978, ISBN 0 913668 58 3, is an introduction to life/work planning. *What Color is Your Parachute?* is an annual guide to career planning and job hunting.

Personal Power – How to Fulfil Your Private and Professional life, by Jenny Mosley and Eileen Gillibrand. Written for any adult wishing to work on their own self-esteem and energy levels so that they can feel more confident about taking on changes. Available from,

JMC, 8 Westbourne Rd, Trowbridge BA14 0AJ
email: circletime@jennymosley.demon.co.uk
website: www.jennymosley.demon.co.uk

The Artist's Way: A Course in Discovering your Creative Self by Julia Cameron, Pan Books, 1994, ISBN 0 330 343 58 0. A source book for unlocking latent creativity full of insights and activities, many of which can be adapted for the classroom (or even for teachers as creators).

The Work We Were Born to Do: Find the work you love, love the work you do, by Nick Williams, Element Books, 1999, ISBN 1 86204 552 6. A personal exploration of the meaning of work, full of quotes, activities and references which offers alternative ways of thinking about careers education.
email: hello@heartatwork.net
website: www.heartatwork.net

9. Partnership with parents

Building Small Democracies: Implications of the UN Convention on the Rights of the Child for respecting children's civil rights within the family, Children's Rights Office.
Available from Children's Rights Office,
235 Shaftsbury Ave, London WCH 8EL
tel: 020 7240 4449

Child Maltreatment in the UK, by the NSPCC, 2000, ISBN 1 84228 006 6. A major survey of child abuse. Summary available on website:
www.nspcc.org.uk

Empowering parents and teachers: Working for children by Sheila Wolfendale, Cassell, 1992, ISBN 0 304 32380 2. One of her many books on work with parents.

Family Learning: the foundation of effective education, by Titus Alexander, Demos Arguments 15, 1997. Makes the case for supporting families as places of learning and parents as a child's most influential educator. Available from Central Books tel: 020 8986 5488

Full Stop Campaign, launched by the NSPCC in 1999, to combat child abuse and violence. For details and school materials send SAE to NSPCC, 42 Curtain Road, London EC2A 3NH
tel: 020 7825 2500

Home School Policies: a practical guide, by Titus Alexander, John Bastiani and Emma

Beresford. Available from
JET Publications, 67 Musters Rd,
Ruddington NG11 6JB tel: 0115 9845 960

Parenting Education and Support Forum,
Unit 431 Highgate Studios, 53-79 Highgate Rd,
London NW5 1TL tel: 020 284 8370
email: pesf@dial.pipex.com Information on
parenting courses.

Parentline Plus, 53-79 Highgate Rd, London
NW5 1TL tel: 020 7735 1214. Information on
parenting courses.

*Take Care! Self-awareness and personal safety
issues in the primary curriculum,* by NSPCC
and CEDC. A resource pack for use with children. Includes a teachers' guide and 24
activities in four booklets, Taking care of myself; Taking care in my family; Taking care in
my home; and Taking care of my safety, with
a useful list of children's books relevant to
dealing with emotional issues. For materials
send an SAE to NSPCC, 42 Curtain Road,
London EC2A 3NH tel: 020 7825 2500

The Hidden Victims by NCH Action for Children.
Studies the impact of family violence on children and ways of dealing with it, including
the role of statutory services, family centres
and informal support networks.
NCH Action for Children, 85 Highbury Park,
London N5 tel: 020 7226 2033

10. Learning beyond school

Centres for Curiosity and Imagination by
John Pearce, Gulbenkian Foundation, 1998,
ISBN 0 903319 78 0. Describes the work of
children's museums or discovery centres as
places of learning. Full of ideas from which
schools can learn and a list of centres
throughout the country.

Education Extra is a national charity which
provides a wide range of support, resources
and help with funding, including a special
briefing on study support and citizenship.
Education Extra, St Margaret's House,
17 Old Ford Road, London E2 9PL
tel: 020 8983 1061
email: info@educationextra.org.uk
web: www.educationextra.org.uk

*Extending Opportunity: a national framework
for study support,* DFEE, 1998. A free accessible
guide to study support and education out of
school. Includes case studies, answers to
practical questions from schools, legal and
financial issues, useful contacts and publications. Available from DfEE Publications
tel: 0845 602 2260

Kids Club Network also provides support for
out of school learning, childcare and enjoyment.
Kids Club Network, Bellerive House,
3 Muirfield Crescent, London E14 9SZ
tel: 020 7512 2112

Learning beyond the classroom, by Tom
Bentley, Routledge/DEMOS, 1998, ISBN 0 415
18259-x. An extensive look at the challenges
facing education, the changing role of schools
and the "new landscape of learning".

See also Ref 18 and Ref 23

11. Learning values

*All Right at Home? Promoting respect for the
human rights of children in family life* is a
practical guide for professionals working with
parents. Includes fifteen useful activities on
human rights in everyday life. Suitable for in-
service training or older pupils. Available
from Children's Rights Office, 319 City Road,
London EC1V 1LJ tel: 020 7278 8222

Discovering Citizenship by Francine Britton,
CSV, 2000 includes exercises on developing
values. CSV tel: 020 7278 6601

Education in Human Values prepared by June
Auton of the Human Values Foundation. A pack
of over 400 pages of lesson plans, ideas,
illustrations, stories, teachers notes and
other materials for children aged 5-12. The
pack covers core values of truth, love, peace,
right conduct and non-violence.
Human Rights Foundation,
Lower Wallbridge Farmhouse, Dowlish Wake,
Illminster TA19 0NZ tel: 01460 52499
email: edhumanval@aol.com
website: www.ehv.org.uk

The Centre for Citizenship Studies in Education
has a guide to materials, ideas and organi-
sations for values education.
The Centre for Citizenship Studies in
Education, Leicester University,
Queen's Building, Barrack Rd, Northampton
NN2 6AF tel: 01604 37712

The Right to a Future is an activity pack based on the Rights of the Child, clearly for ages 6-16. Available from
Woodcraft Folk, 13 Ritherdon Rd, London SW17 8QE tel: 020 8672 6031
email: folk@woodcrft.demon.co.uk

The Virtues Project is a US project developed by Linda Kavelin Popov, for young people from nursery to 18, aimed at developing 52 virtues from Assertiveness to Unity. Guide and materials available through website: www.virtuesproject.com or publisher, Jalmar Press, email: jalmarpress@att.net website: www.jalmarpress.com

Values, Cultures & Kids: Approaches and resources for teaching about family education, by Dorit Braun et al, Birmingham Development Education Centre, 1991, ISBN 0 7487 0024 2. Provides resources for teachers of child development, parenting and relationship education in secondary schools; or teachers of adults covering stereotyping, identity, parenting and provision for families.

Values Education Resource Book by Stephen Joyce, Ginn, 1994. Relates to Ginn's Reading 360 Series and shows how teachers can use stories with a social or moral content as a starting point for moral and citizenship education.

Vision and Values: a handbook for spiritual development and global awareness by Sally Burns and Georgeanne Lamont, Hodder & Stoughton, 1995, ISBN 0340 64412 5. Offers over 100 activities mainly for primary, on values and ways of reflecting in relation to self, community, the earth and significant life events, with references to all main religions and a non-faith perspective.

You, Me, Us! Social and moral responsibility for primary schools, edited by Don Rowe and Jan Newton, Citizenship Foundation, 1994. Uses stories and pictures to develop moral reasoning around friendship, rules, property, power, difference, community and environment.

12. Emotional literacy

Confidence to Learn, by Noreen Wetton and Michele McCoy. A guide to creating a healthy, happy primary school based on children's views using 'draw and write' research strategies. Contains illustrated ideas for lessons and open-ended activities for researching children's views and building them into policy and practice. Available from Sales and Distribution, Education Board for Scotland,
Woodburn House, Canaan Lane, Edinburgh EH10 4SG tel: 0131 536 5500

Dealing with Feeling, by Tina Rae, is a set of lesson plans for 20 different feelings.
Available from Lucky Duck Publishing,
3 Thorndale Mews, Clifton, Bristol BS8 2HX
tel: 0117 973 2881
email: publishing@luckyduck.co.uk
website: www.luckyduck.co.uk

Emotional Intelligence by Daniel Goleman, Bloomsbury, 1996, provides research evidence about the importance of emotions on learning and outlines several education programmes on emotional literacy for primary and secondary schools.

How Are You Feeling, a health promotion resource for 9-13 year olds offers activities on 'living skills' such as being together, anger and conflict, assertiveness, beliefs and values, self-esteem, plus a leader's booklet.
Available from Woodcraft Folk, 13 Ritherdon Rd, London SW17 8QE, tel: 020 8672 6031
email: folk@woodcrft.demon.co.uk

Smart Moves: Why learning is not all in your head by Carla Hannaford, Great Ocean Publishers, USA, 1995. Shows how the whole body is involved in learning and provides 'brain gym' exercises to stimulate learning.

13. Learning to learn

High/Scope Institute, Research & Development Section, Barnardo's, Tanners Lane, Barkingside, Ilford, Essex. For early years.

Montessori education develops early learning skills by creating a stimulating and challenging environment in which 'the child constructs him or her self'.
Montessori Society and Training Centre,
26 Lynhurst Gardens, London NW3 5NW,
tel: 020 7435 7874

Shared Learning in Action: working towards empowerment by Sue Occleston and Pat King. Details from Shared Learning in Action, 7 Cleavley St, Eccles, Manchester M30 8EB, email: shared.learning@which.net

Steiner education emphasises emotional and social learning through self-directed play, stories, and activities to strengthen children's joy of learning.
Steiner Education, Rudolf Steiner House, 35 Park Rd NW1 020 7723 4400

Teaching as Story Telling: An alternative approach to teaching and learning, by Kieran Egan, Routledge, 1988, offers teachers insights into teaching in ways that children learn.

Teaching Children to Learn covers ten teaching strategies for success in learning, and Teaching Juniors describes how to develop skills needed at Key Stage 2. Both by Robert Fisher. Published by Stanley Thornes, Ellenborough House, Wellington St, Cheltenham GL50 1YD tel: 01242 5779944

The Learning Adventure by Eva Hoffman and Zdzistaw Bartkowicz, Learn to Learn, 1999, ISBN 0 9535387 0 2. A book and CD for primary schools, parents and children. Full of exercises applying insights into learning in an accessible, attractive format. Learn to Learn, PO Box 29, Middlewich, CW10 9FN tel: 01606 832 895

14. Thinking skills

Bookstall Forum, have many other books on teaching thinking. Bookstall Forum, 86 Abbey St, Derby DE22 3SQ
tel: 01332 368039
email: enq@bookstallforum.co.uk
website: www.bookstallforum.co.uk

CASE, Cognitive Accelerated Science Education, are exercises to develop thinking in science, published in *Thinking Science* by Michael Shayer, Philip Adey and Carolyn Yates, 1995, ISBN 0333 4851 22. Ten northern LEAs are working together on new CASE materials to be published by Association for Science Education (ASE).
ASE, College Lane, Hatfield, Herts AL10 9AA
tel: 01707 267411.

Centre for Thinking Skills, Brunel University College, 300 St Margaret's Rd, Twickenham TW1 1PT tel: 020 8891 0121

Good Thinking, Citizenship Foundation, 2000. Three volumes, for Key Stages 3 and 4 and post-16, focus on moral ideas which underpin citizenship, such as rights, responsibilities, jus-

tice, democracy, emphasising critical thinking and engagement. Published by Evans Bros.

Philosophy with Children, by Karen Muris. For primary children from five to twelve. Available from The Centre for Philosophy with Children, Old School Centre, Newport SA42 OTS tel: 01239 820440
email: karin@dialogueworks.co.uk
website www.dialogueworks.co.uk

SAPERE, Society for the Advancement of Philosophical Inquiry and Reflection in Education. Details from Roger Sutcliffe, SAPERE, Stammerham North,
Christ's Hospital, Horsham, Surrey RH13 7NF
tel: 01403 242960
email: 100421.440@compuserve.com

Teaching Children to Think, by Robert Fisher. Analyses approaches to teaching thinking and provides ideas for teachers to use. Published by Stanley Thornes, Ellenborough House, Wellington St, Cheltenham GL50 1YD tel: 01242 5779944

Top Ten Thinking Tactics, for Key Stage 2 and 3, offers cartoon-based materials and a teachers' manual to develop key thinking skills based on the philosophy of Reuven Feuerstein and Matthew Lipman.
Available from The Questions Publishing Co, 27 Frederick St, Birmingham B1 3HH

15. Enquiry and research skills

For more information about students as partners in school improvement, contact Michael Fielding, University of Sussex Institute of Education, EDB, Falmer, Brighton BN1 9RG tel: 01273 877024
email: m.fielding@sussex.ac.uk,
or Louise Raymond, Deputy Headteacher, Sharnbrook Upper School, Odell Rd, Sharnbrook MK44 1JX tel: 01234 782211

Lessons from the field: applying appreciative inquiry, by Sue Annis Hammond and Cathy Royal, Practical Press/Thin Book Co, NY, 1998, ISBN 0 9665373 0 0.
website: www.thinkbook.com

16. Peer education

CSV Learning Together is a UK-wide programme of student tutoring involving over 160 universi-

ties and colleges. Students help school pupils with their studies for one morning or afternoon a week, raising attainment and aspirations. CSV also provides a good practice guide, training video and other resources. Since 1998 Learning Together has provided more specific support for improving reading and writing.
CSV, Freepost, EDO 2163, London N1 9BR tel: 020 713 0560

The Peer Support Forum is hosted by the Mental Health Foundation and ChildLine. For information on schools, trainers and latest developments contact,
The Peer Suport Forum,
Mental Health Foundation, 20 Cornwall Terrace, London NW1 tel: 020 7535 7400
web: www.mentalhealth.org.uk/peer/forum.htm

The PeerAid Book by IBIS Trust and Community Service Volunteers (CSV) gives project profiles from 35 schools, guidelines on setting up a peer aid project, advice on training and information on evaluation.
Available from CSV, Freepost, EDO 2163, London N1 9BR, tel: 020 713 0560

Peer Tutoring: A Guide to Learning by Teaching by Sinclair Goodlad and Beverley Hirst, Routledge, 1989. Provides an extensive overview and bibliography of peer education, with a useful checklist and guide to practice for many different approaches with all ages.

17. Mentoring

National Mentoring Network, Charles House, Albert St, Eccles, Manchester M30 0PD
tel: 0161 787 8600
email: natment@globalnet.co.uk
website: www.nmn.org.uk

The Art of Mentoring, by Mike Pegg, Management Books 2000, 1999. An accessible business-orientated guide to mentoring
tel: 01285 760722
email: mb2000@compuserve.com

18. Project learning

Project learning is a skilled activity that benefits from experience, training and support.

Changemakers is supported by the DfEE and the Changemakers charity. It identifies fourteen enterprise skills, from working in a team to presentation skills, with training materials available for each skill.
Changemakers, 45 Somers Road, Welham Green, Herts AL9 7PT tel: 01707 263080
website: www.changemakers.org.uk

Community Enterprise Education in schools and colleges, by Barbara Merrill, CEDC, 1992. A training manual providing an overview, activities and case studies of community enterprise in schools.
CEDC, Woodway Park School, Wigston Road, Coventry CV2 2RH tel: 024 7665 5700.

Community Service Volunteers (CSV), Freepost, EDO 2163, London N1 9BR tel: 020 713 0560, provide an extensive range of materials to guide students and teachers through active learning:
- *Absolutely No Limits* is a handbook for community volunteering schemes in schools, including case studies, presentation materials, guidelines for recruiting, screening and training volunteers, guidelines for mentoring, and advice on evaluating schemes.
- *Discovering Citizenship* is a coherent programme of practical ideas for experiential learning through activities in the school and community. It includes a teacher's manual, student guide and teacher training manual. A two year pilot programme in one inner city school showed an 80% improvement in pupils' behaviour, 40-55% increase in attendance (to 90%), a reduction in exclusions and demonstrable benefits to pupils, the school and community.
- *Chemistry of Change: Primary Schools and Community Enterprise in Cleveland,* by Jim Mulligan, describes the work of 12 primary schools which developed community projects that were integral to the curriculum, strengthened relationships with the community, gave students responsibility and had long term benefits.
- *Community Enterprise in Camden,* 1994, is a case study of one primary and three secondary schools using a community enterprise approach to environmental and business initiatives
- *No Limit: A blue print for involving volunteers in schools* provides practical guidelines for encouraging and supporting volunteers to help in schools.

Durham University Enterprise and Education Unit, Mill Hill Lane, Durham City DH1 3LB tel:

0191 374 2228, have materials for schools, including:

- *Enterprising Educators,* a one year in-service training package for school staff, covering learning styles, teaching approaches, the whole curriculum and case studies.
- *Working for Myself* is an accredited programme at NVQ Level 3 in Business Planning and GNVQ Keys Skills Advanced level, which take students from having no idea of what enterprise to do, through developing an idea, drawing up a plan, negotiating to birth and survival.
- *Active Environmental Learning* is a resource pack for Key Stage 2, covering recycling, sound pollution and the natural environment.
- Materials for an enterprising approach to English, Geography, History, Maths and Technology.

Social Invention Workshops Manual is a programme of 10 two-hour sessions designed to help pupils identify problems at school, in the neighbourhood or personal lives and then address one or two problems. It follows a five-steps cycle of problem identification, idea generation (or brain storming), action planning and carrying out the project and evaluation. Available from, Institute for Social Inventions, 20 Herber Rd, London NW2 6AA
tel: 020 8208 2853

Tools for Self Reliance collect, sort and refurbish tools for developing countries and have a handbook which includes information about the countries supported.
Tools for Self Reliance, Unit A, 47 Allcroft Road, London NW5 4NB tel: 020 7284 1311
or Netty Marsh Workshops, Southampton
SO4 2GY tel: 01703 8689697

Traidcraft supplies goods from developing countries on a fair trade basis, so that the producers get a larger proportion of the income than from commercial companies. They also provide information about the producers and their countries, as well as a substantial education pack,
Just Enterprise. Traidcraft Exchange, Kingsway, Gateshead NE11 0NE tel: 0191 491 0591

19. Political understanding

Council for Education in World Citizenship (CEWC) produces materials on citizenship including *Towards Citizenship Support Pack:*

Materials for 14-19 year olds, and materials linking citizenship, modern foreign languages and science.
CEWC, Sir John Lyon House, 5 High Timber St, London EC4V 3PAL tel: 020 7329 1500
email: info@cewc.org.uk
website: www.cewc.org.uk

Education for Peace, edited by David Hicks, 1988. A collection of essays on the issues principles and classroom practices for learning to create a better world. Includes chapters on conflict, war, peace, justice, power, gender, race, environment and futures.

NewsWise is an internet and multimedia resource based on topical news stories designed to improve literacy and thinking skills of children between 8 and 14 years old. Six half-termly editions are published on the internet, which has an archive of stories from January 1998. email: enquiries@dialogueworks.co.uk
website: www.dialogueworks.co.uk/newswise

UNICEF-UK has primary and secondary resources on children's rights, much of it free.
'Put It To Your MP', UNICEF Education Department, Africa House, 5th Floor, Kingsway, London WC8 tel: 020 7405 5592
website: www.unicef.org.uk/education

Chapter 6: **Taking part: creating a learning democracy**

20. Circle time

Jenny Mosley and colleagues offer a wide range of training resources for primary and secondary school to support whole-school approaches to self-esteem, behaviour and personal development, including;
- *Turn Your School Around,* 1993
- *Quality Circle Time in the primary classroom,* 1996, over 200 activities
- *More Quality Circle Time,* more activities using puppets and objects, with guidance on evaluation
- Quality Circle Time in Action, video with reception class and year six
- *All Round Success,* 100 ideas for self-esteem
- *Junior Citizenship* are videos showing case studies of primary schools
- *Quality Circle Time in the Secondary School:*

A Handbook of Good Practice, 1999.
- *Here We Go Round,* Jenny Mosley and Helen Sonnet, Postive Press, 2000. A book working with 3 to 5 year olds who wish to meet the Early Learning Goals through the Quality Circle Time Model.

Available from, JMC, 8, Westbourne Road, Trowbridge BA14 0AJ tel: 01225 767157 email: circletime@jennymosley.demon.co.uk website: www.jennymosley.demon.co.uk

Lucky Duck Publishing have an extensive range of books and resources including:
- *Magic Circles: Building Self-Esteem through Circle Time,* by Murray White. Two files of activities covering motivation, resisting peer pressure, coping with change and difficulty, prejudice and bullying
- *Six Years of Circle Time: a primary curriculum,* activities from years 1 to 6
- *Picture This: Guided Imagery for Circle Time,* an audio tape and activities book with stories and exercises for primary schools
- *Circle Time Resources* by George Robinson & Barbara Maines
- *Circle Time: an activity book for Teachers; Developing Circle Time; Coming Round to Circle Time* (video) by Teresa Bliss & Jo Tetley

Available from Lucky Duck Publishing, 34 Wellington Park, Clifton, Bristol BS8 2UW tel: 0117 973288 email: publishing@luckyduck.co.uk website: www.luckyduck.co.uk

21. Pupil or student councils

Children's Voices in School Matters, by Laura Ashworth, ACE, 1995. A survey of nearly 200 schools showing good practice in pupil participation. A School Councils information pack is also available from the Advisory Centre for Education (ACE), 22 Highbury Highbury Grove, London E5 tel: 0171 354 8318 email: ace-ed@easynet.co.uk

Junior Citizenship Videos, Inspiring short films on Student Councils and more. From Team Video. Tel: 0208 960 5536

School Councils UK for training courses, videos and materials, including:
- *The School Council Starter Pack.*
- *Citizens from the Classroom: learning by doing,* a short guide to councils.
- *Caring for our School and our Friends - A*

School Council Experience, 20 minute video of Windsor primary school in Toxteth, Liverpool, showing how the council challenges gang behaviour and enables the majority to assert a positive influence on a disruptive minority.
- *Voice of Reason,* Lipson Community College
- *Pupil Councils: An independent monitoring programme* by Michael Khaleel,
- *Growing up with Pupil Councils,* by Teddy Gold. An information pack

Schools Council UK, 57 Etchingham Park Road, London N3 2EB tel: 020 8349 2459 email: flo@scocon.demon.co.uk website: www.schoolcouncils.org

22. Student participation in and beyond school

Article 12 is the only UK-wide organisation run by and for children and young people under 18. It produces a newsletter, holds an annual conference and runs projects. Article 12, 8 Wakley St, London EC1V 7QE tel: 020 7843 6026, email: info@article12.uk.com, website: www.article12.uk.com

Birmingham Youth Parliament website: www.ypp.org-uk

Empowering Children and Young People by Phil Treseder, Save the Children. A training manual for professionals working with young people in a variety of settings, including schools, local authorities and voluntary organisations. It includes case studies and exercises for professionals on the nature and benefits of empowerment, and overcoming barriers to it, and exercises for young people themselves. Details from Save the Children, 17 Grove Lane, London SE5 8RD tel: 020 7703 5400 website: www.oneworld.org/scf/

Hear! Hear! Promoting children and young people's democratic participation in local government, by Carolyne Willow, Local Government Information Unit; *Citizenship: challenges for councils* by Kathy Baker, Institute for Citizenship and Local Government Information Unit. Available from LGIU, 22 Upper Woburn Place, London WC1H OTB email: info@lgiu.org.uk website: www.lgiu.org.uk

Kirklees IYCE Initiative, Kirklees Metropolitan District Council tel: 01484 221157

Manchester Young People's Council
website: www.manchester-ypc.org.uk

Organising Bureau of European School Student Unions
(OBESSU), Nieuwezijds Voorburgwal 21-11, NL-1012RC Amsterdam, Netherlands
tel: +31 (0) 20623 47 13

Running a Youth Council by Andrew Thompson. Provides information sheet and profile of Aylesbury Youth Council. Available from
Shell Better Britain Campaign,
Victoria Walks, 21a Graham St,
Birmingham B1 3JR tel: 0121 212 9221
email: enquiries@sbbc.co.uk

The Euridem Project: A Review of Pupil Democracy in Europe, by Lynn Davies and Gordon Kirkpatrick, Children's Rights Alliance for England, 2000,
Children's Rights Alliance for England,
319 City Road, London EC1V 1LJ
tel: 020 7278 8222
email: info@crights.org.uk

Youth Planet,
105 rue Lafayette, 75010 PARIS
tel: +33 (0)1 53 20 02 05 email:
info@youthplanet.org

23. Taking part in global decision making

Council for Education in World Citizenship
(CEWC) - materials on global citizenship.
CEWC, 15 St Swithin's Lane, London
EC4N 8AL tel: 020 7929 5090
email: info@cewc.org.uk
website: www.cewc.org.uk

Development Education Association is a national umbrella for local centres providing materials and support for global education. Also provides materials, guidelines and training.
DEA, 29-31 Cowper St, London EC2A 4AT
tel: 020 7490 8108
email: devedassoc@gn.apc.org
website: www.dea.org.uk

One World Trust, runs an annual global education competition and provides speakers, including MPs who belong to the All Party Group for World Government. Also promotes Charter 99, the campaign for global democracy.
One World Trust, 7 Millbank, London SW1P,
tel: 020 7219 3825
email: owt@parliament.uk
website: www.charter99.org

Oxfam has produced a Curriculum for Global Citizenship and other materials.
Oxfam Education Unit, 4th Floor,
4 Bridge Place, London SW1V 1XY
tel: 020 7931 7660
website: www.oxfam.org.uk/coolplanet

Peacechild International, The White House, Buntingford, Herts, publishes attractive materials written, illustrated and edited by young people from all over the world, working in partnership with adult professionals. These include:
• A World in Our Hands: A Young People's History of the United Nations, for children over 12
• Stand Up for Your Rights: A Children's Book of Human Rights, for 10-15 year olds
• Pachamama: Our Earth, Our Future, for 11-14-year-olds, includes an introduction to environmental issues, based on the authoritative UN GEO-2000 report

Plan International provides materials about population and demographic issues worldwide,
tel: 01483 755155
website: www.plan-international.org/uk

UNA-UK, a national voluntary organisation with local branches, organises model UN General Assemblies and other meetings, and produces various activity packs to enable others to organise them.
UNA-UK, 3 Whitehall Court SW1A 2EL
tel: 020 7930 2931/2

UNIC, the UN Information Service, also organises MUNGAs and provides free materials on the UN.
UNIC, 21-24 Millbank SW1P 4QH
tel: 020 763 1981
email: info@uniclondon.org

UNICEF-UK provides a catalogue of free resources. UNICEF-UK, Africa House, Kingsway, London WC2B
tel: 020 7312 7613
web: www.unicef.org.uk/education/resources

24. Class meetings

'Dialogue' is an excellent game for class meetings to enable parents to get to know each other, breakdown barriers and understand how children learn at home and in school. Available in primary and secondary versions, from Anne Currie, Department of Education, 8 University Gardens, University of Glasgow, Glasgow G12 8QQ

See also Ref 9

CASE, The Campaign for State Education, produces an informative newsletter, briefings and research papers on parents and schools, as well as conferences and campaigns. Details from: CASE, 158 Durham Road, London, SW20 0DG tel: 020 8944 8206 email: tulloch-case@mcr1.poptel.org.uk website: www.mandolin.demon.co.uk/case.html

25. Community participation

Community Education Association is a network of schools and individuals concerned with community education. It organises conferences and produces a newsletter. CEA, Ernulf, Barford Rd, St Neots, Cambs PE19 2SH tel: 01480 216803 email: comedas@btinternet.com

Community Education Development Centre is the national centre for community education, providing consultancy, training, publications and projects. It also organises a National School and Community Network. CEDC, Woodway Park School, Wigston Road, Coventry CV2 2RH tel: 024 7665 5700 website: www.cedc.org.uk

Learning Towns, Learning Cities, DfEE, 1998, ISBN 0 85522 836 9. Summary of the issues involved in creating a learning town or city, with 17 examples. Free from 0845 6022260. A handbook, Practice, Progress and Value, is available from 0114 259 3207

School Inclusion, by Mog Ball, Joseph Rowntree Foundation, ISBN 1 85835 041 0, An overview of relationships between schools and their communities, identifying good practice, ideas and recommendations for community schools.

The Centre for Participation offers practical guides, support and information for effective participation: Centre for Participation c/o NEF, Cinnamon House, 6-8 Cole St., London SE1 4YH, tel: 020 7407 6473, email: info@neweconomics.org website: www.neweconomics.org

The Schools Funding Guide: what you need to know, by Nicola Eastwood, Anne Mountfield & Louise Walker, The Directory for Social Change, 2000, ISBN 1 900360 57 8. A guide to strategies, the law and sources of money from trusts, government and companies. Directory for Social Change also provide a wide range of training and information on fundraising across the country. Directory for Social Change, 24 Stephenson Way, London NW1 2DP tel: 020 7209 5151 email: info@dsc.org.uk, website: www.dsc.org.uk

Transforming schools through community education by Christopher Bowering-Carr et al, is a study of the characteristics of the best community schools that help pupils achieve high standards, produced by the International Leadership Centre at the University of Hull for Community Education Development Centre (CEDC), available from CEDC (above).

Children have a right to education on the basis of equal opportunity.

Article 28, UN Convention on the Rights of the Child

Endnotes

1. David Hargreaves, *The Challenge for the Comprehensive School*, Routledge, 1982

2. David Hargreaves, *The Challenge for the Comprehensive School*, Routledge, 1982

3. *Education for Citizenship and the teaching of democracy in schools*, (The Crick Report), QCA, 1998

4. Michael Barber, TES 12 Feb 1999

5. *The review of the national curriculum in England: Consultation Materials*, QCA,1999

6. *Tom Bentley, Learning beyond the classroom*, DEMOS, 1998

7. Michael Barber, *The Learning Game: Arguments for an education revolution*, Gollancz 1996/Indigo 1997

8. David Hargreaves, *The Mosaic of Learning: Schools and Teachers for the Next Century*, Demos, 1994

9. David Hargreaves, *The Mosaic of Learning: Schools and Teachers for the Next Century*, Demos, 1994

10. *The review of the national curriculum in England: Consultation Materials*, QCA,1999

11. *Family Household Survey 2000*, HMSO

12. *Education for citizenship and the teaching of democracy in schools, Final report of the Advisory Group on Citizenship,(The Crick Report)*, QCA, 1998

13. Charles Handy, *Beyond Certainty*, Hutchinson,1995

14. Michael Rutter et al, *Fifteen Thousand Hours: Secondary schools and their effects on children*, Open Books, 1979

15. *Changing our School*, Highfield Junior School, 1999

16. Priscilla Alderson, 'Human rights and democracy in schools: do they mean more than "picking up litter and not killing whales"?', *The International Journal of Children's Rights 7*, 1999

17. Lynn Davies and Gordon Kirkpatrick, *The Euridem Project: A Review of Pupil Democracy in Europe, Children's Rights Alliance for England*; 2000; Centre for Educational Research and Innovation, *Parents as Partners in Schooling*, OECD, 1997,

18. *Changing our School*, Highfield Junior School, 1999

19. *Changing our School*, Highfield Junior School, 1999

20. *Changing our School*, Highfield Junior School, 1999

21. Marshall B Rosenberg, *Nonviolent Communication*, Puddle Dancer Press, 1999

22. P Alderson, *Civil Rights in schools, Children 5-16 Research Programe*, School of Comparative Social Sciences, University of Hull

23. *Attitudes to Learning '98, MORI Staate of the Nation Survey: Summary Report*, Campaign for Learning 1998

24. John Holt, *Learning All the Time: How small children begin to read, count and investigate the world without being taught* (1989) Education Now, 1991

25. Jeremy Bernstein, *Albert Einstein and the Frontiers of Physics*, OUP, 1996

26. Richard J. Gelles, *Intimate Violence in Families*, Sage, 1997

27. *The Hidden Victims: Children and Violence*, NCH Action for Children, 1994

28. *Children and Violence*, Gulbenkian Foundation, 1995

29. *Children and Violence*, Gulbenkian Foundation, 1995

30. Richard J. Gelles, *Intimate Violence in Families*, Sage, 1997

31. John Holt, *Learning All the Time: How small children begin to read, count and investigate the world without being taught*, Education Now, 1991

32. *Welcome to Our School: Partnerships with Parents in Partnership -Learning from Newall Green Nursery and Infant School*, Newall Green School, 1998

33. Gordon Wells, *The Meaning Makers: Children Learning Language and Using Language to Learn*, Hodder & Stoughton, 1986

34. *The School Book: life at a comprehensive school*, Peers School

35. Kieran Egan, *Teaching as Story Telling: An alternative approach to teaching and learning*, Routledge, 1988

36. Daniel Goleman, *Emotional Intelligence*, Bloomsbury, 1996

37. Matthew Lipman, *Philosophy Goes to School,* Temple, 1988; John Dewey, *Democracy and Education,* Macmillan, 1916; Vygotsky, *Thought and Language,* 1962

38. Howard Gardner, *The Unschooled Mind,* Fontana Press, 1993

39. *Education for Citizenship and the teaching of democracy in schools (The Crick Report),* QCA, 1998

40. Aileen McKenizie, *Citizenship in Schools: a baseline survey of curriculum & practice,* UK Committee for UNICEF, 2000

41. Joanna Moorhead, *Kids rule,* Guardian Education, 24 October 2000

42. Jessica and Teddy Gold, *Citizens from the Classroom,* Schools Council UK, 1998

43. Bernard Trafford, *Participation, power-sharing and school improvement,* The Educational Heretics Press,1997

44. *Changing our School,* Highfield Junior School, 1999

45. *Child Maltreatment in the UK,* NSPCC, 2000

46. *The Big Picture,* Mental Health Foundation, 1999

47. Titus Alexander, *Family Learning: Foundation of effective education,* Demos, 1998

48. David Hargreaves, *The Challenge for the Comprehensive School: Culture, Curriculum and Community,* Routledge, 1982

49. Based on an account by Steven Andrews in *The Democratic School,* Edited by Clive Harber and Roland Meighan, Education Now, 1989

50. Mog Ball, *School Inclusion,* Joseph Rowntree Foundation

51. Third Sector Alliance, Carlingcott, Bath

52. Fiona Carnie, Martin Lange & Mark Tasker (eds), *Freeing Education: Steps towards real choice and diversity in schools,* Hawthorn Press, 1996,

About the Author

Titus Alexander is an independent educator and author who works in all phases of education. As a research assistant at Sussex University he developed a course on Learning to Learn. He taught current affairs for many years and was a community worker in Brighton and London, a Principal Lecturer in the ILEA and then General Adviser (Community Education) for the London Borough of Waltham Forest. He is co-author of Riches Beyond Price: Making the Most of Family Learning, which coined the term 'family learning'; and Home-school Policies: A practical guide. He edited The Self-Esteem Directory: a guide to policy and practice, 1997. Other publications include Know University, 1976; Value for People: adult education and popular planning, 1986; and Unravelling Global Apartheid: an overview of world politics, 1996.

He is an Associate of the Global Commons Institute, Development Education Association, National Children's Bureau, and National Home-School Development Group; a founder member of the Parenting Education & Support Forum and of the Self-Esteem Network. He is also a maker and teller of stories for children of all ages.

Learning Initiatives
32 Carisbrooke Road
London
E17 7EF
titus@gci.org.uk